VANCOUVER ISLAND SCOUNDRELS,
ECCENTRICS AND ORIGINALS

Vancouver Island Scoundrels, Eccentrics and Originals

TALES FROM THE LIBRARY VAULT

Stephen Ruttan

GREATER VICTORIA
PUBLIC LIBRARY

TouchWood
Editions

TouchWood Editions
touchwoodeditions.com

Originally published in 2013 by the Greater Victoria Public Library.
First TouchWood edition, 2014.

LIBRARY AND ARCHIVES CANADA CATALOGUING IN PUBLICATION
Ruttan, Stephen, 1947–, author
Vancouver Island scoundrels, eccentrics and originals: tales from the library vault / Stephen Ruttan.

Co-published by: Greater Victoria Public Library.
Reprint. Originally published: Scoundrels, eccentrics and
originals: Victoria, BC : Greater Victoria Public Library, 2013.
Includes bibliographical references and index.
Issued in print and electronic formats.
ISBN 978-1-77151-072-1

1. Swindlers and swindling—British Columbia—Vancouver Island—History—Anecdotes.
2. Swindlers and swindling—British Columbia—Victoria—History—Anecdotes. 3. Eccentrics
and eccentricities—British Columbia—Vancouver Island—History—Anecdotes. 4. Eccentrics
and eccentricities—British Columbia—Victoria—History—Anecdotes. 5. Vancouver Island (BC)—
History—Anecdotes. 6. Victoria (BC)—History—Anecdotes. I. Ruttan, Stephen, 1947–.
Scoundrels, eccentrics and originals II. Greater Victoria Public Library, co-issuing body III. Title.

FC3846.25.R88 2014   971.1'2   C2013-907183-0

Editor: Judy Moore
Proofreader: Sarah Weber
Design: Pete Kohut
Cover image: Victoria, 1951, Walter J. Phillips, oil on canvas
(from *Cities of Canada: The Seagram Collection*)

We gratefully acknowledge the financial support for our publishing activities
from the Government of Canada through the Canada Book Fund, Canada
Council for the Arts, and the province of British Columbia through the
British Columbia Arts Council and the Book Publishing Tax Credit.

This book was produced using FSC®-certified, acid-free paper,
processed chlorine free and printed with vegetable-based inks.

2   3   4   5   18   17   16

This is for Judy Moore. Without her drive, energy, and enthusiasm, this book would never have happened.

—Stephen

CONTENTS

છ૭ છ૭ છ૭

Preface

STEPHEN RUTTAN'S *Vancouver Island Scoundrels, Eccentrics and Originals: Tales from the Library Vault* is, just as the title promises, an account of scoundrels, eccentrics and originals that populate the history of Victoria and Vancouver Island. Stephen has an eye for great stories and a lively knack for telling them. Here he has collected tales, some short and some tall, of real people (plus a ghost and a sea monster) whose colourful lives have left their traces in the "vault" of the Greater Victoria Public Library. Some were notorious: Brother XII, the absconding cult leader, or Stella Carroll, Victoria's preeminent brothel keeper. Others were eccentric: the newspaper pioneer and early premier Amor de Cosmos, or the socialite Victoria Jane Wilson who left her fortune to a parrot. And then there were those, like the Aboriginal man Jimmy Chickens or Francis Rattenbury, designer of the two landmark buildings on the book's cover, who were both eccentric and notorious. The twenty tales told include those of the white slave of the Nuu-chah-nulth, of the Chinese lepers of D'Arcy Island, and of the black pioneer who went on to become a judge and consul to Madagascar.

While I can't swear that the stories of the Cadborosaurus or all the other tales are "strictly true" or provable, I can say that each is an engaging window into the fascinating history of Vancouver Island from the arrival of the first explorers in the 1780s, through the 1850s when the death of a pig brought Britain and the United States to the brink of war, to the sensational love-triangle murder of Victoria's most famous architect in 1935. By allowing this peek into the vault of the Greater Victoria Public Library, this book has opened the island's past and invited everyone all to explore it more deeply. Thank you, Stephen!

John Lutz
Department of History
University of Victoria

Louis the Parrot.

Miss Wilson
and the Parrot

LOUIS THE PARROT NO LONGER rules the roost in Victoria. Once, he was the most famous media personality in town and had a man-servant to tend to his every need. He ate walnuts, hard-boiled eggs, and brandy, and lived on a prime chunk of downtown real estate.

Magazines such as *Life* regularly ran stories about him. The estate he lived on was his and could not be developed while he lived. There were those who saw him as standing in the way of progress.

But Victorians liked Louis. They liked his regal lifestyle and his thumbing his nose at the way of "progress." They were happy to see him live out his long life in splendour. This was some recompense, they felt, for the sad life his mistress had had to live.

Louis's story is really that of Victoria Jane Wilson, who acquired Louis when she was still a little girl. She was born in 1877 in Victoria. Her father, Keith Wilson, was a real estate tycoon, and her mother, Mary, was descended from early fur traders in Victoria. Growing up, Victoria Jane had a comfortable, but very closeted, existence.

Her father, for reasons best known to himself, did not want her to meet strangers, especially men. Perhaps he thought fortune hunters would try to grab her.

Whatever the reason, her seclusion became something of a scandal in Victoria.

James Nesbitt had a story to tell about this. As a boy, he would deliver newspapers to the Wilson household. Victoria Jane was there every day to get the paper from him. But she rarely said a word. No wonder, for fifty feet away stood her father, glowering at the paperboy. As Nesbitt said, he was standing there "making sure that the paperboy did not run after his daughter."

On the few occasions when Victoria Jane did leave the house, her father would follow her. He would be hovering in the background, occasionally dodging behind poles if she happened to talk to someone. No wonder she grew up to be a painfully shy recluse.

Birds became her true love. Enter Louis. She was given Louis when she was five, and he quickly became the love of her life. Many other birds followed. Over the years, she bought budgies, love birds, Panamanian parrots and various other species.

Eventually, her aviary was one of the largest of its kind in Victoria. It occupied the entire top floor of her house. But no matter how many birds she acquired, Louis always remained her favourite. He was, in fact, the major impetus in her one attempt to break free.

In the early 1900s, she bought a Hupp Yeats electric car. She wanted to learn how to drive and take Louis for a spin. She did take a few driving lessons. But Louis didn't take to motor cars. He didn't like the noise, and the fumes irritated his skin. So, sadly, the car went into the garage for good. By the time she died, the car had become sealed in the garage, and a wall had to be knocked down to get it out.

The story of Louis the Parrot became internationally famous.
This photo of Louis with his caretaker appeared in *Life* magazine.

As the years wore on, her parents died. First her mother went in 1917. Now Victoria Jane had to look after her father. But seclusion had taken its toll. Long before her father died in 1934, she had become a full-fledged recluse, seldom going out or seeing people.

She did ease up a bit after his death. Nesbitt reports that she gave small, intimate dinner parties at the Empress and the Priory. She also liked to go on the occasional shopping spree for clothes and perfume. But it was too little, too late.

When Victoria Jane died in 1949, it was discovered she had an unusual bequest in her will. She left a substantial sum for the care of her birds. No institution would take them, so her lawyer decided they would be best off if they were left just where they were.

The bird who has it made

Canadian Feb 10, 1969 P 19.

Louis is a parrot with cradle-to-the-grave security – thanks to the provisions of a wealthy Victoria, B.C., spinster's will. And he's still going strong – at 102   BY DESMOND BILL

LOUIS NO LONGER controls the best piece of property in downtown Victoria, B.C. Nor does he any longer have a personal manservant to attend to his needs. He doesn't even get the daily tot of brandy he was said to be swilling.

But he is still the most pampered, best protected and certainly the most famous parrot in Canada, if not the world.

Yet nobody knows where Louis lives, except a very conservative Victoria law-

Louis likes brandy – in moderation.

She was a hoarder and, at her death in 1949, her house was found to be packed with clothes, some of which she apparently had never worn. There were stockings that had never been taken out of their tissue paper, hundreds of hats, huge piles of foundation garments, and closets full of dresses.

But the real surprise was a clause in her will concerning Louis. She left about $200,000 each to the Red Cross and Victoria's Royal Jubilee Hospital, and $20,000 each to the B.C. Protestant Orphanage and the city's Queen Alexandra Solarium for Crippled Children. But she also specified that a portion of her estate should be used for the care of her aviary – then containing about 60 birds of various species – and what was left after the death of the last bird should be divided between the Red Cross and the Royal Jubilee Hospital.

The lawyer knew that Miss Wilson's main concern had been to care for Louis. Since there were no facilities at that time for housing the birds locally, he decided to maintain the aviary on the property to a developer, he made it a condition that the aviary be leased back for a nominal sum.

This effectively prevented any developer from levelling the house and using the site and its spacious grounds for a

says the lawyer, Louis got brandy only when he was sick. "I can remember buying only three or four bottles of brandy for him in almost 20 years," he says.

He shared this house with 60 macaws, pheasants, parrots and budgies.

parts of the estate were given to the hospital and the Red Cross.

The lawyer said he made the change because it was no longer economical to operate the aviary. And he knew Wong

Louis in *Canadian*, February 10, 1969.

Her former servant, Wah Wong, was paid to take care of the birds. The Wilson property was sold. But the lawyer made it a condition that the house be leased back to the estate, so the birds could keep their home. This, of course, made it impossible to develop the property. The property changed hands several times, but the birds remained.

Over the years, the birds died, and eventually Louis was the only one left. But parrots live far longer than humans. No one knew exactly how old Louis was, but it was a sure bet that he would outlast all the humans around him. And he was definitely the favourite.

Eventually, a solution was found. In 1966, seventeen years after Victoria Jane's death, Louis went to live with Wong. Money was provided for his care. And with Louis gone, the developers were free to develop the estate.

A big new hotel was built on the site of Louis's former home. For a few years, there was a restaurant on top of the Chateau Victoria called the Parrot House. But times change and memories fade.

Not long after the transfer, Wong died. While the family continued to care for Louis, he must have missed his friend. The Wong family would not talk, but there was a report that a few years later, Louis, too, had died. And, bowing to fading memories, the Parrot House changed its name. Louis, it would seem, was gone for good.

A good story, though, never dies. Who knows? Louis himself might still be around.

Postscript

The Hallmark Society is an organization dedicated to heritage preservation in the Capital Regional District. It has named its most prestigious honour the Louis Award, in memory of Louis and his demolished home. The award recognizes an exceptional heritage building restoration, one that demonstrates unusual attention to authenticity and structural integrity, and that has had an exemplary impact on a neighbourhood or region. As it recognizes only the truly exceptional, it is not awarded every year. The recipients are given something Louis would have approved of: walnuts and brandy.

The remains of a creature, possibly a young cadborosaurus, found in the stomach of a whale.

Caddy the Cadborosaurus

WHEN HUBERT EVANS SAID HE had seen a sea serpent, people believed him.

After all, Evans was one of the most highly respected writers in British Columbia. Born in 1892, he lived most of his life at Roberts Creek, north of Vancouver. While mainly a novelist, he knew wildlife well and wrote extensively on the subject. He was also known for his exceptional honesty and integrity. So when he told fellow writer Howard White the amazing thing he had seen, White gave him the benefit of the doubt.

In an article in *Raincoast Chronicles*, Howard recounts Evans's story. One day in 1932, Evans and another man were working on a road. A neighbour came running up, urging them to come and see something. They were looking at a strange sea creature through a telescope. It was dead calm on the water, in the sunny glow of a late afternoon. Through the telescope they could see a series of bumps on the water. "Sea lions," said Evans, "They run in a line like that."

"Just keep watching," said the neighbour. And then, at the end of the bumps, a shaft six or eight feet high shot straight up into the air. Comparing it with a spar buoy out on the water, they estimated it as twelve inches wide. "Could be a log," said Evans, casting around for a credible explanation. But then this "log" started to elongate horizontally, and they could see a head resembling a horse's. This head then turned, and seemed to look straight at them. As Evans said, "It just put the hair up on the back of your neck."

They wanted to record this, but had no camera with film. So Evans stopped looking and went back to his job. His daughter, though, continued to watch the creature as it swam along the coast. They all knew they were looking at something unusual, but nobody wanted to talk, knowing they would be laughed at and would risk their reputations if they reported what they'd seen. So they kept quiet. Evans himself rarely mentioned it.

What Evans and his friends saw was probably a "cadborosaurus" (or "Caddy" for short). This term was created by a Victoria newspaper in 1933 when a strange local sea creature came to its attention. The paper reported that in October of that year, Major W.H. Langley, clerk of the provincial legislature, and F.W. Kemp, an employee of the provincial archives, and their families were sailing off Chatham Island. They saw, not more than one hundred feet away, the dome of a creature's back breaking the surface of the water. It was the size of a large whale, but in other respects entirely different. It was a dark greenish brown, with serrated marks along its back and sides.

The creature disappeared quickly, but it prompted Mr. Kemp to recall a similar incident. It had happened at approximately the same area in the previous year, in a narrow channel with steep rocks on one side. As he was watching, a "creature shot its head out of the water on to the rock, and moving its head from side to side appeared to be taking its bearings. Then fold after fold of its body came to the surface." Its body, toward the rear, "appeared serrated, like the cutting edge of a saw." Its movements "were like those of a crocodile." It had a sort of mane around its head, which drifted about the body. He estimated the creature to be at least sixty feet long and about five feet thick.

There have been dozens of sightings of this creature since the nineteenth century, many by knowledgeable observers. There is a remarkable consistency to their descriptions. It has a long, snake-like body, with an elongated neck. Observers are often struck by the appearance of the head, which is variously described as horse-, giraffe-, or camel-like. It has vertical humps on its body and is a very fast swimmer. It is propelled by a split tail and often (but not always) has a serrated back.

In all its characteristics, the cadborosaurus resembles no known creature. In fact, as Paul LeBlond and Edward Bousfield write in their book *Cadborosaurus: Survivor from the Deep*, "a visual comparison of Caddy with other major marine contenders [sharks, sea lions, etc.] illustrates how strikingly different it is." But it still has not received scientific recognition. Because of a lack of hard physical evidence it remains a "cryptid," or a creature whose existence is officially in doubt. Until an actual specimen or carcass comes along, it will probably remain that way.

Undoubtedly there have been many misidentifications over the years. As was noted in the Evans story, a travelling herd of sea lions could be mistaken for a multi-humped creature. Basking sharks are another possibility. They bask on the surface of the water, are up to forty feet in length, and look like rough-barked logs. Now almost extinct in BC waters, they were once quite common. Some Caddy sightings have proven to be basking sharks. But there are two encounters that are hard to dismiss.

One day in 1937, a sperm whale was brought in to the Naden Harbour whaling station. When the flensers cut into the whale's stomach, they brought out a strange animal. They were familiar with everything a whale normally ate, but they had never seen anything like this. Its long, slender body, tail, and horse-like head are all consistent with descriptions of a cadborosaurus. Photographs were taken of the creature and confirm that this could have been a young cadborosaurus. The carcass was shipped off to the Pacific Biological Station in Nanaimo, but unfortunately it has since disappeared.

In the second incident, writer William Hagelund tells of catching a baby cadborosaurus just off De Courcy Island. Hagelund was a former whaler and knew sea life extremely well. This was like nothing else he had ever seen. He made a careful examination of it, and his description and drawing fit well with descriptions of Caddy. He kept it in a water-filled pail, intending to take it to the Pacific Biological Station. But the creature thrashed around in the pail and was obviously very agitated. Hagelund knew it would probably not survive. So he let it go.

So just what is a cadborosaurus? The long, thin body with movements like a crocodile would suggest it is a reptile. The absence of layers of fat would make it cold-blooded, like fish and reptiles. Unlike fish it is an air-breather, which means it must surface periodically. Sightings have suggested it can hold its breath for a long time, which is a mammalian characteristic. Also mammalian is the likelihood that it bears live young. It would seem, then, that Caddy is a reptile, with some mammalian characteristics.

An artist's vision of a cadborosaurus.
COURTESY OF TIMOTHY DONALD MORRIS

Its closest relatives would be extinct marine reptiles, such as early seagoing crocodiles. It certainly wouldn't be the only sea creature to survive from the age of the dinosaurs. The coelacanth, a fish thought long extinct, was caught off the east coast of Africa in 1938. Human knowledge of sea animals has really barely begun, and many surprises will be encountered in the ocean depths in the years to come.

Although not much is known about Caddy, that hasn't stopped the local community from having a relationship with him. He is depicted in the art of Native people, and there are stories of him in West Coast Native folklore. There are numerous reports of sightings from early settlers. But the moment when Caddy really came into public consciousness was in 1933.

Earlier that year, the Loch Ness monster became big news in Britain. That gave colonial papers, such as those in Victoria, licence to follow suit. So when Major Langley and company reported their sighting, the *Victoria Daily Times* made it front page news. The newspaper's managing editor, Archie Wills, made it his personal mission to publicize Caddy. The competing paper, the *Daily Colonist*, at first tried to ignore it but was forced to join in. They even tried to control the issue, by renaming the creature "Amy" Cadborosaurus. But "Caddy" prevailed.

With all the publicity, the number of sightings soared. Newspapers in North America and Europe picked up the story, and cartoonists had a field day. The tourist industry loved Caddy, and the Chamber of Commerce was his greatest defender. It seemed as if Victoria had been just waiting for a sea monster.

But the euphoria did not last. After the 1940s, sightings dropped off. There was a low of six sightings in the 1970s, but the numbers climbed higher in the 1980s and 1990s. Like many other animals, cadborosaurus may be suffering from the effects of too many people, and declining in numbers.

Caddy is not the publicity engine he once was. Many Victoria residents today, if asked about Caddy, would respond with a blank look. But the reality of the sightings cannot be denied. Over the years too many knowledgeable and observant people have seen this creature unlike any other. Caddy will probably remain in the consciousness of people living in Victoria, and sightings will continue to occur. But he remains a mystery—perhaps for the better. As John Steinbeck once said, people "really need sea-monsters in their personal ocean . . . an ocean without its monsters would be like a completely dreamless sleep." Caddy's presence in the ocean is a reminder that there will always be realms and creatures beyond humans' imagination.

Missing Since Tuesday

Victor Gravlin and his wife, Doris Gravlin, missing from their respective homes since last Tuesday, are being sought throughout Greater Victoria. Mr. Gravlin is described as being in his middle-thirties, about five feet eleven inches tall, weight about 135 pounds, medium build and of a nervous temperament. Mrs. Gravlin is thirty years of age, five feet six inches tall, weighing 130 pounds, with auburn hair, and large brown eyes. Last Tuesday she was wearing a knitted dress, blue coat with silver buttons, and a grey hat.

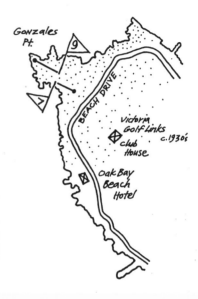

Newspaper article, left, reporting the Gravlins missing (*Daily Colonist*, September 27, 1936). Map of the golf links, right, where the ghost appears.

COURTESY OF RHONDA BATCHELOR

The April Ghost of the Victoria Golf Links

DRIVING THROUGH THE VICTORIA GOLF Club's course at night can be an eerie experience. The city, with all its lights and buildings, is a few miles away, and in this dark and wind-swept area, all that can be heard are the sounds of the wind and the pounding seas. It is a setting of bleak loneliness, with hardly a living person to be seen.

Once this course was the site of a violent murder, and it is now the home of Victoria's most famous ghost.

The story begins in 1936. Doris and Victor Gravlin were a young couple living in Victoria. She was thirty, he was in his mid-thirties. They had a seven-year-old son called Walter, according to newspaper reports of the time, but he was later known as Robin.

Victor Gravlin had worked as a sports reporter for the *Colonist* newspaper until illness (possibly alcoholism) forced him to quit in 1934. Doris worked as a private nurse for an older lady. Their marriage had been going badly and by September of 1936 they were living apart. However, they were still attached to one another, and on

Tuesday, September 22, 1936, they arranged a meeting to discuss a reconciliation.

Just what happened that evening will never be known. Both were last seen about 8:00 PM, as Victor left his home and Doris her place of work. The Victoria Golf Club course was an obvious place to meet, as they had often enjoyed walking from there to the Oak Bay Beach Hotel. No one saw them after that, and the two were reported missing by their respective parents a few days later. On the following Sunday, a caddy discovered the beaten and strangled body of Doris on the beach. Victor Gravlin had disappeared.

The search was now on for Victor. Several municipal forces, the provincial force, and even a boy scout troop were involved. A month later, he was found.

A fisherman discovered his body floating offshore, tangled in a bed of kelp. Doris's shoes, missing from her body, were found stuffed in his pocket. The case was reported as an obvious murder-suicide and everyone felt it was resolved.

Everyone, that is, except Doris herself. Within months people began reporting her appearance on the golf course. Here is a description of one of the first reports of her, taken from Charles Lillard and Robin Skelton's pamphlet *The April Ghost of the Victoria Golf Links*:

A fisherman fishing off the rocky shore of Gonzalez Point, the section of the Victoria Golf Links containing both the seventh green and the ninth tee, was one of the first Victorians to see Doris Gravlin after her death. The fisherman was unable to say what made him turn around and look up the bank and the green. But he did, and there, standing above him, was a woman staring out towards the kelp beds.

She paid him no attention whatsoever, even though she was only a few feet away.

He could not immediately understand why she was there. Theirs was not an easy place to reach, nor was this a spot where women walked by themselves. The light was fading fast and all the fisherman noted, besides the gloomy look on her face, was what he later described as "an old-fashioned brown suit." The suit stuck in his mind because Oak Bay was, then as now, one of Victoria's richest suburbs, and hardly the place where young women ignored fashion. He continued casting. She said nothing. He said nothing, and "then she suddenly hurried down as if she was going to meet someone, and on the way she vanished. I saw her kind of melt away."

Over the years there have been many sightings of Doris. Why she became known as the "April" Ghost is a mystery. She has appeared in various months, late March being the commonest.

She prefers two areas, and two times of day. Between 4:30 and 5:00 PM she strides through the golf course looking like a normal person, except for her old-fashioned clothes. Between 9:30 and 10:00 PM, the most common time to see her, she appears at the green closest to the water, looking decidedly more ghostly.

She will appear with arms out-stretched, wearing a long white gown. She will rush toward people, then disappear. She also exhibits a variety of other behaviours.

One night, for example, a man saw her as he was out walking on the course. He turned around and then turned around again, and she was facing him every time. After completely boxing him in, she disappeared.

Supernatural Vancouver Island–1

THE APRIL GHOST
OF THE
VICTORIA GOLF LINKS

Charles Lillard & Robin Skelton

Supernatural Vancouver Island––1

Cover of the *April Ghost* pamphlet, written by Charles Lillard and Robin Skelton.

On another night a woman was out walking the course with a group. A wild wind suddenly sprang up, blowing at them from all directions, despite it being a perfectly calm day. Some of the group became very frightened. As the woman hung back from the rest of her group, she felt someone with a cold, clammy hand take her hand. She assumed one of her friends needed comforting. Then she noticed that all her group had moved on, and she was alone. The hand then disappeared.

There have been many such stories over the years. With over seventy years of haunting she has become easily the most famous of local ghosts. She has entered the imaginative landscape, thanks to writers such as Charles Lillard and Robin Skelton being attracted to her story.

But what of her future? Will she continue to haunt the shores of Victoria, or will she move on? Her son has had something to say about that. Overlooked in most accounts is the seven-year-old boy she left behind. He was adopted by his grandparents, became known as Robin Thomson, and went to school in England. He later joined the British Army and had a military career.

Robin seldom came back to Victoria. When contacted by a reporter in 1994 for a comment about his mother's ghost, he was completely surprised. He knew next to nothing of the tragic events and asked for more information on them. When contacted next, though, he was philosophical about it. He said, "If it's history, then it's there, and it's not going to go away."

Two Chinese lepers on D'Arcy Island.

The Lepers of
D'Arcy Island

BOTH BIG D'ARCY AND LITTLE D'Arcy Islands, off the east coast of Vancouver Island near Victoria, are heavily forested and have a lovely, peaceful appearance. This certainly belies their miserable past.

From 1891 until 1924, these islands were home to a lazaretto, or leper colony. People who were discovered to have leprosy were simply exiled there, with no possibility of reprieve.

The lazaretto was established by the municipal council of Victoria in 1891 in response to five Chinese lepers being discovered in a shack in Chinatown.

The traditional horror of this disease moved the council to action. Leprosy, or Hansen's disease as it is formally called, is an ancient curse of mankind. It goes back as far as recorded history, and probably beyond. It is caused by a bacterium and is not very contagious. People living in close and unsanitary conditions, though, can contract it much more easily. It can take many years to manifest itself.

What it does makes the horror understandable. The bacterium

damages the body's peripheral nervous system. The victim then loses the sense of pain. In consequence, he or she can be injured or infected and not be aware of it. Also, the body is greatly disfigured. Plaques can develop on the skin, while other parts of the body can wither away.

Strange physical appearances are common, such as faces with leonine (or lion-like) characteristics. Fingers and toes disappear. Tissue in the body can swell. When the swelling occurs in the nose and throat, breathing is more difficult, and patients can even suffocate. So fear of this disease is fully justified.

The city councillors knew leprosy would frighten the public, so they had to act. The first thing they did was to request, from the provincial government, the use of D'Arcy Island. On April 22, 1891, this was granted. A few days later, a local paper reported that it would be useful for a "garbage crematory." Obviously the council was trying to avoid panic. But soon the truth was out.

On May 5 there was an article in a local paper about the proposed colony. By then preparations were in full gear. On May 13, men and materials were taken to the island to construct the necessary buildings. These had already been designed by architect John Teague. On May 20, everything had been prepared, and the lepers were ready to be sent.

To judge from the local newspaper, the citizens approved. The headline in the *Daily Colonist* on May 21, 1891, reads: "Effectual measures taken to prevent leprosy becoming rooted in Chinatown," and goes on to say: "The five lepers of Victoria [will be] properly isolated." The lepers themselves are horrifyingly depicted: "More repulsive human beings would be hard to imagine. Each was a total physical wreck, and their features were so distorted, disfigured and swollen as to be almost out of human semblance." The article goes

Artist Don Gill's notebook on D'Arcy Island.
COURTESY OF DON GILL

on to describe the excellent facilities that have been created for the victims, and finishes by saying that "the city authorities will visit the lepers periodically and see that their wants are supplied."

No mention is made of any medical care for the lepers. There was none. Desperately sick people were simply being dumped on an island and left to fend for themselves.

The lepers knew what was in store for them. The same article says "all of them made strenuous objections to leaving the city." They dreaded their fate so much that "a guard was placed over the house on Fisgard Street where they had been living" to prevent them from escaping. One attempted suicide. They knew their lives were effectively over. Whether or not they liked it, the lepers were sent to D'Arcy. For fifteen years they lived alone on the island. The only exception was when a new sufferer joined them. The lepers would be visited by a supply ship every three months, with a medical officer along for a checkup. They had to get their own water, which was sometimes seriously lacking. If someone died between visits, no one in the outside world would know of it.

Ironically, there already was a lazaretto in Canada, where the sufferers were treated well. It was in New Brunswick and was an actual hospital for lepers. The federal government ran it, and had the necessary medicines to alleviate the suffering. The Victoria city government wanted the federal government to take charge here as well, but it refused. Expense was probably not an issue, since there were few lepers involved. But there was another factor. The patients in New Brunswick were Caucasian. Those at D'Arcy Island were all Chinese, and by the 1890s, prejudice against the Chinese was strong.

In 1897, Dr. R.L. Fraser became chief medical officer. In 1899, he wrote that the lazaretto was "in a truly deplorable condition." Only one of the six lepers was able to work. The rest were in various states of debilitation. He implored the federal government to take over.

Other medical men voiced strong concerns. A report in a medical journal in 1898 by doctors Ernest Hall and John Nelson made clear how bad the situation was. But an even more graphic presentation was in a letter from Dr. Ernest Hanington of Victoria.

Writing to Sir William Osler, Canada's most prominent medical figure, he said: "I have been to the island twice, and it was a very painful experience." He catalogued the numerous problems on the island, and then described his final parting from the lepers: "The wretched beings, some in the last stages of the disease . . . lined up on the beach and cried like children when we were leaving."

What finally forced a change in the D'Arcy situation was pressure from the BC government. It pointed out that the federal government was allowing Chinese immigration and collecting a substantial head tax from the immigrants. Since the federal government was not allowing the BC government any veto, it should at least share some of the tax money. This could then be used to treat the lepers. The federal government agreed. In 1905, it gave some money, and services on D'Arcy improved.

This seems to have been the prod for the federal government to move. In 1906, it passed the Leprosy Act and took over operations on D'Arcy. The colony now changed completely. It became a true medical facility, with a new attitude toward the lepers. The policy now was to repatriate as many as possible. In 1907, all residents were sent back to China. Seven were placed with the Presbyterian Mission to Lepers in Canton. The eighth chose to return to his family. New buildings were erected on D'Arcy, and it was now set to deal with new leprosy cases.

Supplies for the lepers were regularly sent by steamer from Victoria.
IMAGE C-03858 COURTESY OF ROYAL BC MUSEUM, BC ARCHIVES

A handful of new cases came in over the years, but there were fewer residents than before. Now that there was a policy of repatriation, D'Arcy was merely a detention centre for some, until a steamship could be found to send them home. The few who stayed there had a resident caretaker and a Chinese interpreter. They also had the necessary medicines to alleviate their suffering.

This was the situation until 1924, when it was decided that D'Arcy was no longer needed. A new station was opened on Bentinck Island, near the quarantine station at William Head. The five remaining lepers were transferred there, and the colony on D'Arcy Island was closed for good.

D'Arcy looks much the same today as it would have then. It is beautiful and tranquil, and a favourite destination for boaters. But there are strong reminders of the past. Artifacts from the colony have been found on the island, and burial mounds can still be seen in the bush. There is a bronze memorial, placed by the City of Victoria. The Parks Branch has also remembered the lepers, erecting a pictorial display of their lives.

Being reminded of what happened to the unfortunate lepers banished to D'Arcy Island is important. Nothing can be done to right these wrongs. It is perhaps wishful thinking to say such abuse could never happen again. But if the memory has prompted people to examine how poorly some humans treat others, then those who died on the island will not have died in vain.

Chinese businesses on Fisgard Street.

Chinatown Myths
and Realities

CHINESE IMMIGRANTS WERE EARLY ARRIVALS in Victoria. The first record of their arrival is from 1858, when a group from San Francisco came to join the gold rush. Along with thousands of others, they came in search of gold in the Cariboo. But some saw opportunities here in Victoria. They stayed and the formation of Chinatown began.

From its beginning in the area of Cormorant (now Pandora) Street, Chinatown grew over the years as thousands of immigrants arrived from China. The Canadian Pacific Railway had a huge need for labour—as did coal mining and other industries. Chinatowns had developed in many towns and cities in North America, but Victoria's was easily the largest. It was physically separate from the rest of the community. Because it was on the north side of the Johnson Street ravine it could be reached only by three narrow foot-bridges. This changed over the years as Victoria and its Chinatown grew. But the sense of separateness remained. It was to remain a factor in relations between residents of Chinese and European origin well into the twentieth century.

In his book *The Forbidden City Within Victoria*, David Chuen-yan Lai examines why Chinatown was so remote and mysterious to the white community. It was composed, for the most part, of young, single men who spoke little English. The cultural gap between them and the Caucasian population was very wide, and members of the Chinese community were frequently persecuted. They were, for example, the target of frequent police raids. Consequently, the Chinese community felt they needed a "forbidding" Chinatown to protect themselves. The result was a community physically and psychologically impenetrable to Victoria's white community.

New World Chinatowns were modelled on the old villages of China—narrow, meandering alleys and inner courtyards were common features. This provided a familiar environment and a sense of protection for the Chinese residents. But it also gave rise to prejudice: newspapers of the time warned white Victorians that "Criminals could be lurking in any dark alley" and "Your money and your life would be at risk." "Women should not walk there alone," it was said. Chinatown engendered both fear and a morbid fascination in outsiders.

Out of this fascination two major legends arose. One is the myth of tunnels in Chinatown. To some members of the Caucasian community it appeared that Chinese fugitives could easily escape pursuers down dark alleyways, into hidden courtyards, and through doors that led in many directions. Hence the myth arose that there must also be tunnels underneath Chinatown. In fact, because some Chinese residents had been involved in the opium business, a legend arose that they had a tunnel to the harbour for smuggling purposes. Members of the

CANADIAN
Illustrated News

VOL. XIX.—No. 17.   MONTREAL, SATURDAY, APRIL 26, 1879.   SINGLE COPIES, TEN CENTS.
$4 PER YEAR IN ADVANCE.

THE HEATHEN CHINEE IN BRITISH COLUMBIA.

AMOR DE COSMOS, ESQ.—The Lover of the World or the Lover of Mankind.—HEATHEN CHINEE:—Why you sendee me offee !
A. D. C.:—Because you can't or won't 'assimilate' with us.—HEATHEN CHINEE:—What is datee ?—A. D. C.:—You won't drink whiskey, and talk politics and vote like us.

A reflection of white attitudes to the Chinese in late nineteenth-century BC.
The man in the top hat is Amor De Cosmos, second premier of the province.

Street scene in Victoria's Chinatown.
IMAGE B-03974 COURTESY OF ROYAL BC MUSEUM, BC ARCHIVES

Caucasian community would point to an outlet on the harbour as the exit for this tunnel. In truth, it was an outlet for the storm drainage system. But the myth persisted, and a discovery in the 1950s renewed it. A very large cistern was discovered buried under Store Street. Speculation arose that this was part of the tunnel network. It was not: this cistern and others discovered since were part of Victoria's early fire-fighting system. There is no credible evidence these supposed tunnels ever existed.

A second legend arose about Chinese tongs. The word "tong" means "meeting place" and is loosely applied to many kinds of Chinese associations. A clan association and a charitable organization are both examples of tongs. To the Caucasian imagination, fed on cultural misunderstandings, these were sinister organizations. Lurid stories in the local press would dwell on tong violence and warfare.

There were, of course, occasional conflicts within the Chinese community. Tong membership might exacerbate a situation if a whole tong lent its support to an individual's dispute. And there were disputes and animosities from the old country that were carried over into the new. David Chuen-yan Lai mentions, for example, a long-running feud between the Taishan and Hakka peoples, who had fought for many years in China and carried the dispute to the New World. But this was really no different than the violence happening within other ethnic groups new to Canada. The history of the Irish Fenians in the early years of post-Confederation Canada, and their assassination of D'Arcy McGee, serve as reminders of that.

Rockwood, the most palatial brothel Victoria has ever seen.

Stella: When Only the Best Will Do

PROSTITUTION IN VICTORIA PROBABLY BEGAN with the founding of Fort Victoria.

After the gold rush and the growth of the city, gradually brothels emerged in Victoria to serve different clientele. The highest-quality houses were around Broughton and Courtney streets. They catered to society's upper crust, such as members of the nearby Union Club, and were not raided by the police.

The bulk of the sex trade, though, was conducted farther north. Herald, Chatham, and Fisgard streets were the heart of the red-light district, with some brothels also on Broad and Johnson. Here the sailors, workmen, and others further down the social scale could be entertained. Business boomed in the nineteenth century. Even in 1891, there were far more men than women in Victoria, and something of the frontier prevailed.

On to this scene came Stella Carroll. Born in Missouri, she had grown up in the rough-and-tumble American West. By age twenty-five, with two failed marriages behind her, she went to San Francisco to seek her fortune. Opportunities for women were much fewer than they are today, but one business had great possibilities. Brothels were traditionally run by women and were in high demand.

She was not interested in being a prostitute herself. She wanted to run the show. Fate intervened for Stella. In 1899 she went to visit her friend Vera Ashton, who ran a brothel in Victoria. Vera was about to sell her business to another woman named Marval Conn. But while Stella was there, Conn had a terrible accident and died. While upset at this death, Stella had the sense to realize that this was an opportunity. Taking Vera aside, she proposed to step in and conclude the purchase. Vera agreed, and Stella became the proprietor of a fine, two-storey establishment in the Duck Block on Broad Street.

Stella was lucky that her new landlord was Simeon Duck. He was a well-connected local politician with a liberal attitude to prostitution. With protection from him, she made the house even finer. Her furnishings were always meticulous, and she did much of the housekeeping herself. Few could meet her standard. She ran the establishment like a boarding house, with the girls paying her rent. They kept the proceeds, while Stella made her money on the sale of liquor.

Things went well for the next few years. With Duck's protection she had minimal interference from the police and could concentrate on running the business. But Duck died in 1905 and, unluckily for Stella, there was a rising tide for "moral reform" in the city. Politicians were being forced to control prostitution. In 1906 a reformer, Alfred Morley, was elected mayor. He and the police chief had a meeting with Stella, where they struck an unofficial deal. If Stella would move her business out of downtown and over to Herald Street, the de facto

Stella Carroll.

red-light district, the police would not trouble her. This way the mayor could be seen as tackling the prostitution problem, without upsetting the demand for this service. So Stella made the move. But citizens' groups and a local newspaper continued to demand moral reform. The authorities were forced to renege on their deal, and the police continued to raid Stella's operation. Angry though she was, Stella was forced to recognize the new reality. She began to think of leaving the business entirely.

In 1908, however, a new opportunity arose. Rockwood, a beautiful mansion and estate on Gorge Road, was up for sale. As well as being a superb place for a high-class brothel, it had two advantages. First it was in Saanich, which meant that Stella could escape from the Victoria police. Second, it was on the Gorge Waterway, so customers could arrive discreetly by boat.

Stella bought it and set to work to make it the finest brothel Victoria had ever seen. Expensive furnishings from Europe, oriental rugs, nothing was too good for this house. Stella's own appearance set the tone. She wore dresses of hand-made lace from Ireland, and diamonds in her hair. Her undergarments were tight and uncomfortable but gave her a regal and commanding appearance. For entertainment, she had an excellent piano player and a new phonograph. And of course she had the best girls. She had truly fulfilled her dreams.

But, sad to say, troubles continued to dog her. Moral reform, whether it was directed at sex or alcohol, was a movement sweeping North America. It would culminate in Prohibition in the 1920s. But some of Stella's problems were her own doing. Unlike the downtown houses, she was still being raided by the police. The difference was the owners of those houses were quiet and discreet, with good political ties.

Stella was always the flamboyant outsider. She would, for example, sue a non-paying customer in court, when good sense should have told her not to. When the police arrested her and hauled her into court, she would rage at the magistrate. And her private life caused problems. She had violent lovers, one of whom shot her in the leg, which then had to be amputated. She herself was known on occasion to hit a girl. In a still very British town, this was not the accepted norm.

Her worst problem, though, was not her doing. Her long-time lawyer and confidante, Todd Aikman, betrayed her. He accepted the job of Saanich prosecutor and was thus in the position of taking Stella to court. With Aikman knowing all her business secrets, Stella no longer found Saanich the safe haven it once was.

Stella began to think of leaving Victoria. After a few more stormy years, she went to visit her friend Tessie Wall in San Francisco. There she discovered that Tessie was leaving the profession and was selling her business. Stella bought it, and left Victoria in 1913. Except for a brief visit a few years later, she left for good.

But business in San Francisco was difficult as well. Moral reform groups were as active there as they were in Victoria. Also, Stella's friend Tessie had become emotionally erratic and would not leave the house. The end was in sight. When the First World War was over, Stella decided to leave the sex trade. Tired and ill from her leg, she became the landlady of a boarding house.

The remaining years of her life were happy, then sad. She married a decent man, and had twelve good years of marriage. As well, she was close to her siblings and enjoyed entertaining her nephews and nieces. But her husband died in an accident, and the insurance company refused to pay up. In her last years Stella was penniless and lonely.

The route to Rockwood for visitors arriving by boat.
COURTESY OF LINDA EVERSOLE COLLECTION

Her family were a comfort though, and she would make notes in her scrapbook of her wonderful memories. She died in 1946.

People seeing her in these last years could scarcely have imagined the rich life she had had. They are not alone. Until recently, people could not easily find information on her. The GVPL, for example, has no clipping files on Stella Carroll. This changed three years ago, when Linda Eversole published her book *Stella: Unrepentant Madam*. It introduced a fascinating and important member of Victoria's past, a past people are only now willing to acknowledge. Today Stella can be seen as a pioneer businesswoman, someone who overcame the handicaps of poverty and being a woman in a man's world. Prostitution was one of the few opportunities a woman had, and she made the most of it. She had the misfortune to live in an oppressive era, but she dealt, usually successfully, with the obstacles in her path. Her recognition is long overdue, and Eversole is to be thanked for bringing Stella's story to light.

Postscript

Stella's beloved Rockwood burned down in 1923. The Duck Block however, where Stella had her first brothel, still stands on Broad Street. Also still standing is her brothel on Herald Street, which now houses the Youth Hospitality Training Centre. This centre offers temporary housing and skills training for youth at risk. Stella was very fond of young people and was known for helping those in distress. Her own childhood had been very hard, and she would have empathized strongly with those needing help. The centre serves as a fitting memorial to her.

Jimmy Chicken Island.
COURTESY OF STEPHEN RUTTAN

Jimmy Chicken.

Jimmy Chicken

GROWING UP IN OAK BAY in the 1950s, I had never heard of Mary Tod Island. I knew, of course, the island that lay just off the shore near the Oak Bay Boathouse. I passed it every day on the way to school. But no one ever called it "Mary Tod." For everyone, it was simply "Jimmy Chicken." I had heard vaguely that the name referred to a Native man who had lived on the island. But I knew nothing more.

The name, though, was strange. How was it that in white, well-off Oak Bay, a landmark would be named for a Native man? Native place names are not unusual on the coast, but those named for specific Native individuals are. Jimmy Chicken, though, was not a "usual" person. Indeed, he was one of the most colourful individuals in early Victoria.

Jimmy and his wife, Jenny, lived on Mary Tod Island in the latter part of the 1800s. To them, the island would have been "Kohweechela," which means "where there are many fish."

Fishing was Jimmy's main occupation. One of his customers was John Virtue, who ran the Mount Baker Hotel on the Oak Bay waterfront.

Mount Baker Hotel on the Oak Bay waterfront, where Jimmy Chicken sold fish.

This was Jimmy's main source of income, but not his only way of making a living. He acquired his surname from his habit of stealing chickens. According to one observer, Jimmy would "snatch a chicken and make a run for it, scuttling down to his canoe . . . and paddling like fury . . . to his little island."

Despite this, he was well liked. He was a genial, pleasant person, even when drunk, which was much of the time. He and his wife would go on frequent binges, and, as one writer put it, "many a noisy carousal echoed across the water to Oak Bay." Sometimes, if he was drinking in town and the winds were too strong to paddle back to his island, he would simply curl up by a roadway for the night. He obviously had a tough constitution, because he was well over sixty by the time he died in 1901.

The people who knew him best were the police. So often did they pick him up and put him in the drunk tank that he was the most frequent occupant of their cells. He was always genial and so trustworthy that they would let him out to run errands.

His son Johnny would usually come to visit him, bearing a change of clothing and some words of comfort.

In 1899, Jimmy's wife died. Jimmy was inconsolable with grief, and for a time stopped drinking altogether. But then he started carousing harder than ever. He also came up with a solution to his loneliness. He stole a young Songhees woman (her age was not recorded) and spirited her over to his island. She was not there long, though. Four of her tribesmen came racing after her. Jimmy lost her, and nearly lost his own life in the ensuing fracas.

Although Jimmy was something of a figure of fun to the white population, he seems to have been a man of stature in the Native community. When he died, to quote one writer, "At least 100 canoes [were] drawn up on Oak Bay Beach, where the Native people went through their ceremonial dances to the beat of drums. The body was then taken aboard a large canoe and the whole armada took off for Chatham Island. There Jimmy was buried with further ceremonies."

This incident points to a real problem with the information on Jimmy's life. The documents on him are, of course, written entirely from the white perspective of a century ago. As such, they embody the prejudices of the time. Colourful details are recorded, but not those that would bring him into focus as a fully functioning adult of another culture.

Few details are available about this interesting character, other than that he was a fisherman who stole chickens. Unfortunately, nothing is known of Jimmy Chicken's Native name, the languages he spoke, or his spiritual beliefs.

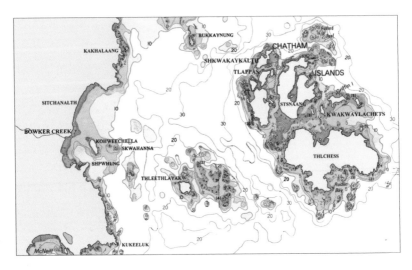

Map showing Jimmy Chicken Island.
COURTESY OF GRANT KEDDIE

Ironically, this was not the case in the remote Queen Charlotte Islands. There, at the same time, John Swanton was recording major works of literature from Native informants. Here in Victoria, in the white community, there was little interest in Native culture on its own terms.

Fascinating details occasionally pop up in the records that are available. One report says Jimmy was originally from the Cowichan area. He does seem to have behaved differently from other Native people around white people, and perhaps an outsider status might explain that.

Another detail is the house he lived in. One article described it as "like the old-time Indian house." Since Jimmy was probably born before the founding of Fort Victoria, he would have learned to build in a traditional Native style. If he was from farther north, would he have designed his house differently from local houses? No photographs exist that could answer this question.

John Virtue, proprietor of the Mount Baker Hotel and friend of Jimmy Chicken.
IMAGE A-02512 COURTESY OF ROYAL BC MUSEUM, BC ARCHIVES

Another intriguing detail is the bride-stealing incident. Bride theft is a well-known practice among other ethnic groups. Although it was hilarious to the white people, was Jimmy Chicken, in fact, just following an accepted norm for his own community? Anthropologists may be able to answer this question, but what his community actually was is unknown.

Sealing schooners in the Inner Harbour, Victoria.
IMAGE G-0111 COURTESY OF ROYAL BC MUSEM, BC ARCHIVES

Alex MacLean.
COURTESY OF CAROL BROOKMAN

The Sea Wolf

Pacing back and forth the length of the hatchway and savagely chewing the end of a cigar was the man whose casual glance had rescued me from the sea . . . my first impression . . . was . . . of his strength . . . a sinewy, knotty strength . . . a strength we are wont to associate with things primitive . . . a strength that was excessive and over-whelming.

SO BEGINS THE DESCRIPTION OF Wolf Larsen in Jack London's novel *The Sea Wolf*. Larsen is captain of a sealing schooner in the North Pacific, who with his physical and mental strength rules the ship with an iron hand. He seems a simple brute, but in fact he is a highly intelligent man with intellectual interests. But he lives as a virtual savage on board his ship and despises the refinements of civilization. His crew are similiarly tough, and life aboard the ship is basic and primitive.

London created this character and in doing so mythologized the sealing industry and its frontier way of life. But many claim that Wolf Larsen was not a creation. Rather, they say, he was modelled on the life of a real sealing captain, Alex MacLean. Based in Victoria in the 1880s, MacLean could well have been London's model. Originally from Cape Breton, MacLean and his brother Dan were legendary for their prowess at catching seals, and for their brushes with the law. Just how wild and brutal Alex MacLean was remains in dispute, with many claiming he was not brutal at all. But there was still truth in London's tale. Sealing in the North Pacific, where a fortune could be won or a life lost easily, was tough and unpredictable. It attracted those who were willing to live on the edge. Someone who thrived in this industry, such as Alex MacLean, was bound to become a legend.

Sealing began in the North Pacific long before MacLean's arrival. The prized species was the North Pacific fur seal, which mostly breeds on the Pribilof Islands in the Bering Sea, off Alaska. A smaller number breed on north Asian islands. When not breeding, these seals roam the open Pacific Ocean.

Russia owned the Pribilofs and began a land harvest in the eighteenth century. Gradually Russian hunters decimated the herds, but restored them as they saw the need for conservation. In 1867 the United States bought Alaska. Without the Russian conservation program in place, an orgy of killing occurred. The US government, waking up to the herd's possible demise, halted the slaughter and then awarded an exclusive contract to the Alaska Commercial Company. This company, beginning in 1870, harvested and managed the seals until 1890.

In British Columbia, sealing began as a small industry on the coast, with Native people selling skins to white traders. It was small because the seals were difficult to catch. Native people were forced to paddle to the open ocean before starting the hunt. In 1868 the trader James Christiansen attempted to change that. He loaded four canoes and twelve hunters on his schooner *Surprise*, then took them out to the sealing grounds. Now the Native people could stay nearby and avoid paddling long distances. The first trip did not go well, but the second one was very successful. The word spread, and the North Pacific pelagic sealing industry was born.

Pelagic sealing (or sea hunting) had been practised for several years when Alex MacLean arrived. He came from a seafaring family in Cape Breton, and arrived on the west coast in 1881. After working at various jobs, he and his brother Dan became active in sealing, an expanding industry in the early 1880s. A technical development that made the removal of guard hairs from seal easy increased the demand. Fur seal coats were becoming very fashionable.

In 1883 the MacLeans, in different boats, made pioneering voyages to the Bering Sea. This was the richest area for pelagic sealing, and Canadian sealers had not gone there before. Both men made substantial catches. In 1884 they went back again and did even better. Alex got 1,754 skins, and Dan 1,954. They went back every year for the next few years. The size of their catches just kept on increasing.

In 1885 they did an experiment. Alex went out in a boat staffed only with Native hunters, Dan in one with white hunters. The idea was to see who would have the most profitable season. Dan caught more skins, 2,309 to Alex's 2,073, but Alex had lower costs, so it was a dead heat.

Whatever the method, the industry kept expanding. In 1886 Alex brought in 3,325 skins, while Dan brought in a record 4,256 skins. Also, the number of boats was expanding. Throughout the 1870s there were always less than 10 boats out. In 1881, though, it was 19, and in 1886 it was up to 38. It peaked at 124 in 1892. Most were American or Canadian ships, but some were registered under different flags, and some were of unknown origin. Most of them sailed out of Victoria.

An inherent conflict in the industry began to erupt. The success of pelagic sealing threatened the size of the land harvest. The American government began to be very concerned about the depletion of what they considered to be "their" resource. In 1886 American revenue cutters began to seize ships in the Bering Sea. They were laying claim to the Bering Sea as American territorial waters. This was in direct contravention of international law, which considered any ship sixty miles or more from land as being in international waters. The four ships seized that season, including one partially owned by Alex MacLean, were all beyond the sixty-mile limit. The British and Canadian governments strongly protested, claiming this was "a blatant violation of traditional rights on the high seas." They were ignored. The Americans stepped up their policy, seizing fifteen vessels in 1887. International tension picked up, and many feared that war would break out.

For sealers, dodging American cutters became a new hazard in their work. They risked losing all their catch and possibly being stranded in Alaska. Sealing was so lucrative they were willing to take a chance. This is when Alex MacLean's "outlaw" reputation began. As well as dodging US authorities in the Bering Sea, he engaged in some activities that seemed suspicious. He would sometimes spend more time than normal in port, or land at unusual locations. In the years to come there were many rumours of his smuggling, gun-running, and poaching activities. Some of the poaching, but not much else, is documented. MacLean tended to avoid the press and not tell people what he was doing. As a result his legend grew, but few facts were actually known. In many ways he is still a man of mystery.

MacLean and his family moved to San Francisco in 1890. He had formed a business relationship with Herman Liebes, who owned a company that dealt in furs. Liebes was particularly good to work for and treated his captains well. MacLean may also have preferred San Francisco. It was a boisterous, free-wheeling city, with lively action in the saloons.

Part of MacLean's legend is that he was a hard-drinking, sometimes pugnacious man. This seems to have been generally true. But that he was, supposedly, a brutal, demonic captain on his ships, terrorizing his crews, is almost certainly false. Anecdotal evidence depicts him as a stern taskmaster, but no monster. One documentary source, the "Red Record," published in the *San Francisco Coast Seamen's Journal*, recorded all reported instances of cruel treatment on American ships. MacLean, who sailed out of San Francisco from 1890 on, never made that list.

In 1891 the British and American governments came to an unexpected agreement. In an effort to calm tensions and conserve the seal population, they agreed to a one-year halt to all sealing in the Bering Sea, both on land and at sea. But it had some unexpected effects. Conservation was not helped, as the sealers turned all their attention to the Asian herds. Their numbers were drastically reduced. Also, since pelagic sealing was allowed outside the Bering Sea, many more seals were killed on the open ocean. Pelt prices were so high, many sealers were willing to risk anything. Consequently sealing became a very rough business. Russians as well as Americans were strongly protecting the seas around their rookeries. Sealers thus had to dodge guards when attempting to hunt for seals in forbidden waters.

In this situation the MacLean brothers took a gamble. They made a coordinated raid on Russian rookeries on Copper Island. But the effort failed. As they began the raid, the Russian guards spotted them and opened fire. Dan MacLean escaped and eventually made it back to San Francisco. Alex was not as lucky. His ship was boarded by the Russians, and he and his crew were arrested. They were taken to Vladivostok.

J.M. Heinold's First and Last Chance Saloon. This was a favourite haunt of Alex MacLean's.
COURTESY OF CAROL BROOKMAN

Alex loudly proclaimed his innocence and demanded a trial to prove it. The Russians ignored him. But he and the crew had the freedom of the city and had to report to the police only once a day. After ten weeks the Russians let them go, and they found a ship back to San Francisco.

The next few years were not easy for MacLean. The prices for fur seal pelts dropped significantly. The Americans had put more ships and resources into patrolling the Bering Sea, harassing the pelagic sealers. This eased up in 1894, but the low prices meant few people made any money. He did some sealing off Japan but had trouble with his Japanese crews. Finally, unusually bad weather frequently made sealing impossible.

The result was that MacLean decided to leave the business. By then it was becoming obvious that the glory days were over. Too many sealers and a declining seal population were making it hard to make any money. Both Alex and his brother Dan had foreseen this. In 1892 they had submitted papers to fur seal arbitration proceedings. In these papers they had claimed that if the situation did not change, the seal industry would soon be finished. Alex gave it ten years, Dan only three. Both stressed the absolute need for more conservation. But whatever conservation was done was not enough. So because of this and other factors, Alex decided it was time to move on.

For the next few years Alex MacLean pursued other ventures. In 1897 he sailed to the South Pacific, hunting for gold in the Solomon Islands. That project failed. Next, he decided to pursue his fortune in the Klondike. He never found gold but saw an opportunity in steamboats. For the next few years he ran paddle wheelers on the Yukon River.

In 1904 he was lured back to the seal industry. It had continued to decline, but seal prices were very high. Also, the Russo-Japanese War, which had just broken out, meant that the Russian seal islands were less protected. A group of four San Francisco investors decided to take advantage. They bought a boat and registered it under the Mexican flag. They did so because Mexico was not a party to any fur seal agreements. Americans were actually forbidden to do any pelagic sealing. This however, did not stop the investors. They hired Alex MacLean to be their captain. MacLean could not legally be a sealer, since he had become an American citizen. But such things did not get in his way.

MacLean and his crew headed to Copper Island to attempt some poaching. But though the Russian navy was absent, there were still guards on the island. When the sealers attempted to land, the guards opened fire. One of the crew, Walter York, was struck by a bullet in the head. They did manage to get him back to the United States, but he died on the operating table. Despite this outcome, MacLean and the investors decided to try again. In 1905 they changed the Mexican registration and gave the boat a new name. They did so because the United States government was starting to investigate. MacLean gathered together a rag-tag crew and headed out to sea. After he left, the government closed in on the investors, arrested them, and indicted them on several charges. As for MacLean, American revenue cutters were instructed to intercept his boat and arrest him.

Ironically, it was a literary event, and not the cutters, that ended his voyage. In 1904 Jack London published his novel *The Sea Wolf.* The lead character, Wolf Larsen, was modelled on MacLean. Initially the press did not make the connection. When they did, though, they went wild. They painted MacLean as a "pirate," roaming the seas beyond the law. All the exaggerated characteristics that were Wolf Larsen's were now MacLean's. It made the sealing expedition impossible. MacLean's crew found out, from newspapers given by passing ships. They decided the game was up. They refused to carry on and forced MacLean to head back to North America. That meant Canada of course, as MacLean would have been arrested in the United States.

He landed at Clayoquot, on Vancouver Island's west coast. This was not a customs port, so he was forced to come to Victoria a week later. He was fined for customs infractions but was not arrested, and did not have to return to the United States. In a way he was lucky, but he was bitter at the press. To a reporter he said, "You've broken up my voyage—that's what you've done. Things were printed in the newspapers about me, and when the crew read 'em they wouldn't seal any more . . . If it hadn't been for the newspapers I'd be sealing yet." He went on to claim his complete innocence.

Regardless of the outcome, though, he wouldn't have been sealing much longer. The opportunities for sealing were just disappearing. Only seventeen ships sailed out of Victoria in 1906, and five in 1909. There were simply too few seals left to catch. In 1910 the main sealing nations, United States, Great Britain, Japan, and Russia, discussed the issue. Canada had some issues about compensation claims and so did not participate. But Great Britain still had international authority for Canada, so it did not matter. In 1911 they established the North Pacific Fur Seal Convention. By this convention all signatories were prohibited from pelagic sealing. The fur seal herds would be allowed to recover. When possible, surplus males would be harvested from the rookeries, with the proceeds being split among the signatories. It was a landmark agreement, and one of the first major international treaties created for wildlife conservation.

MacLean did not long outlive the end of sealing. His family moved up from San Francisco and settled in Vancouver in 1906. He had various maritime jobs, such as operating tugs. At one point he was running explosives up the Skeena River. He drowned in an accident in 1914.

The legends about Alex MacLean have grown over the years, but information about the real man remains elusive. One writer has said that he believes very little of what he reads or hears about MacLean. One reason certainly is MacLean's reticence. He appears to be someone who spoke little about himself, especially to the press. The famous novel has only complicated the matter. The scholar Don MacGillivray has done an excellent job of sorting out myth from reality. But in one sense it may not matter. MacLean, with his alter ego Wolf Larsen, has become a symbol of the sealing life. A tumultuous frontier often spawns larger-than-life characters, who through their exploits define an era. MacLean certainly did his. Not much is known about the real Alex MacLean, but the myth of his life lives on. He highlighted an era and provides a way of understanding it.

Madame Blavatsky, left, theosophist and inspiration to Brother XII (E.A. Wilson),
right, photographed on July 25, 1927, his forty-ninth birthday.

Brother XII

LATE ONE NIGHT A RETIRED sea captain had a vision. Edward Arthur Wilson, a forty-six-year-old Englishman, had retired to the south of France in 1924. In the course of his life he had travelled the world widely and had studied many traditions. He had long been attracted to the mystical and occult. And now, as he lay in bed, he saw a Tau, the Egyptian Cross, hanging in mid-air.

Over the next few weeks Wilson had other visions. He felt he was receiving direction from an ancient Egyptian spiritual master. This master was a member of the "Great White Lodge," a body of advanced spiritual beings who directed the world. Wilson, who was a disciple of theosophy, believed in such masters. Along with other theosophists, he believed certain people can be selected as spiritual leaders. They receive secret knowledge from the masters and impart it to others. Wilson was now such an adept. He felt his master was directing him to a special role in the world. He must follow his master's commands.

Who was this man who was now being given these commands? Little is known of his early life. Born in England in 1878, he left home at an early age. He spent his life at sea, eventually becoming a sea captain. He married a New Zealand woman in 1902 and had two children. They lived briefly in British Columbia, before he abandoned them in 1912. After that, nothing is heard of him until 1924.

Such a bare resumé does not suggest a spiritual leader. But his visions changed him. He knew he had to act on his beliefs and was being directed to do so. His first task was to change his name. The Egyptian master was the twelfth brother of the Great White Lodge. In honour of this, and to show that he was his disciple, Wilson assumed the name "Brother XII."

His next task was much more complex. He was told to write two books, dictated to him by his master. The first was *The Three Truths*, a commentary on three basic truths of theosophy: the unity of all life, the immortality of the soul, and the law of karma. The world's ignorance of these truths was leading to a period of chaos and destruction. The consequence would be a long and painful period of rebuilding.

The second book was an urgent manifesto, *A Message from the Masters of the Wisdom*. In this Wilson reiterated that chaos and destruction were imminent, and that a special "work" was being prepared by the masters, to be conducted in a special "Ark of Refuge." Individuals would be trained in this Ark of Refuge to provide spiritual enlightenment and prepare the world for the coming Age of Aquarius.

Wilson arrived in England in 1926. As well as publishing two books, he had written articles for the leading occult magazine, *The Occult Review*. Having become very well known in theosophical and occult circles, he began to prepare for his life's work. The Ark of Refuge, he decided, was to be established far from England, on the west coast of Canada, and he began to recruit followers. An ad in *The Occult Review* attracted just a few people who were willing to go.

Among them were Alfred and Anne Barley, who were to remain his most loyal disciples till the bitter end. So he set off for Canada.

Wilson, now known as Brother XII, began lecturing to theosophy chapters across Canada. He was very successful and began attracting many followers. He set up an organization, called the Aquarian Foundation, and invited people to join. He also attracted the attention of Joseph Benner, a publisher of astrology and occult books. With Benner's help he started to become well known south of the border.

When Brother XII arrived on the West Coast, he began looking for a place to set up the Ark of Refuge colony. He purchased land on the sea at Cedar, a community just south of Nanaimo. Already substantial contributions were coming in, making such a purchase possible. Next, he began a recruitment drive in California. He had successful speaking engagements in San Francisco and elsewhere. He attracted many new members, and chapters of the foundation were set up in California. Some of the new members were very high-profile. Will Levington Comfort was a well-known writer, and Coulson Turnbull was one of America's leading astrologers. These two, plus Joseph Benner and several others, became founding members of the Aquarian Foundation's first board. Several moved to Canada and lived in the colony.

Brother XII's movement continued to steam ahead. By July 1927, the Aquarian Foundation was able to have its first board meeting. Brother XII's success had been extraordinary. Three years previously he had been isolated, penniless, and unknown. Now he headed a successful organization and had become a prominent personality. But all was not well. Certain aspects of Brother XII's conduct were causing concern. For a number of years he had a "companion" named Elma

Madame Z, Brother XII's notorious mistress.

Wilson, who was regarded as his wife although they were not legally married. But now Brother XII began an affair with a beautiful young follower, Myrtle Baumgartner. What particularly bothered some people was that he was having sex with her in the "House of Mystery," a building that had been built for spiritual contemplation. When the issue was raised, Brother XII claimed that spiritual leaders were governed by different rules. This union was a spiritual union, ordained by the masters of the Great White Lodge. Some people were willing to accept this, but others were not.

Sex was not the only issue. Brother XII had started publishing a magazine, *The Chalice*, and was using it to push an American political agenda. A prominent Catholic, Alfred Smith, was running as the Democratic candidate in the 1928 presidential race. Brother XII was using his magazine to promote an anti-Catholic, anti-capitalist, and anti-Jewish agenda. He thought a powerful third party could be formed, which would be the champion of Protestant America. He also thought that a strong anti-capitalist and anti-Jewish (the two were one in his mind) message could be used to defeat Hoover, the Republican candidate. Brother XII even thought he had a potential candidate, Senator James Heflin of Alabama. But when Brother XII went to the third party conventions, he failed completely in his attempts. He came back to Cedar and tried to downplay what he had done, but some people thought such a message and such activity were not appropriate for a spiritual leader.

But the biggest problem of all was Brother XII's growing authoritarianism, particularly in regard to the foundation's money. He had purchased land at the north end of Valdes Island for the expansion of the colony. Now he was having buildings built on the land, without any discussion with the board. He seemed to think that his will was law. Some followers, such as Will Levington Comfort, saw the drift of things and quit. Others, though, decided to force the issue. They insisted that Brother XII dissolve the Aquarian Foundation. He seemed to acquiesce, then stacked the board meeting in his favour. In response the dissident governors took Brother XII to court, charging him with misappropriating thousands of dollars of the foundation's money. In turn Brother XII accused the foundation's secretary of stealing twenty-eight hundred dollars. The secretary disappeared before his case was finished. And Brother XII was saved by a new American benefactor, Mary Connolly. She insisted to the court that her very large gift was to Brother XII personally, and not to the foundation. The court let him off. Meanwhile the dissolution of the Aquarian Foundation became a political issue for the provincial government to deal with.

The provincial government came into the picture because of a journalist, Bruce McKelvie. He started to investigate Brother XII and the Aquarian Foundation when the court cases began. McKelvie thought he smelled a rat. His interviews and investigations convinced him that this was a cult devoted to free love and the swindling of rich, gullible Americans. He made it his mission to expose Brother XII. As well as publishing articles in his newspaper, McKelvie wrote to his friend Harry Pooley, the Attorney General of BC. He told Pooley of the weird occultism going on at the colony, and of sexual behaviour that was unfit to publish in his newspaper. He urged Pooley to investigate. His message to Pooley was: "We don't want [this] in British Columbia."

Sensational stories from McKelvie and others had the desired effect. Only the provincial Cabinet had the authority to dissolve an incorporated body. They now began to investigate the Aquarian Foundation with this in mind. They were spurred on by a further court case.

Former employees of the foundation were suing for back wages. The issue was not a major one, but during the trial some odd behaviour occurred. The main witness was the former board member Coulson Turnbull. This was a man Brother XII particularly hated for becoming a dissident. Turnbull was strong and healthy, but when sworn in to testify, he began to tremble like a leaf. He then collapsed. Several members of the audience also fainted. The judge tried to adjourn the court, but he found he could not speak. He could only growl like a dog. Finally he managed to utter, "This court is adjourned."

After a while the case resumed. Turnbull recovered but was not strong enough to testify. Then the lawyer for the plaintiffs, T.P. Morton, stood up to summarize their case. But he stood there in confusion. Finally he stammered, "This is ridiculous, but I've forgotten what I was [going to say]." The judge tried to prompt him, but he just stood there confused. With Morton incapacitated, and with insufficient evidence against the defendant, the judge was forced to dismiss the case. Brother XII was around, shaking hands. Many people were convinced he had been practising black magic.

The press covered the case intensively. But even with the negative publicity, the Cabinet took a year to decide the issue. Finally, in November 1929, the foundation was dissolved. Former board members could get title to the properties they had invested in at Cedar, but no assets were attached to the foundation, so Brother XII was free to use any money that had accumulated. And a great deal of money had been coming in, principally from Mary Connolly and other wealthy disciples. He converted much of this into gold coins and packed it away in jars. No one knows how much he stored. But some say it must have been a small fortune. He also acquired a new mistress. In 1929 Mabel Skottowe, a thirty-nine-year-old redhead, arrived at the colony with her husband. Brother XII immediately took up with her, and her husband acquiesced. Brother XII had been in the process of getting rid of Myrtle Baumgartner. He had wanted her to produce an heir, a supposed reincarnation of the Egyptian god Horus. But after two miscarriages that was no longer possible. She was also, not surprisingly, suffering from emotional problems. Some of the women in the colony helped her. But eventually she went back east, and was not heard from again.

At the same time Wilson was getting rid of his "wife" Elma. She still loved him, despite everything she had had to put up with. But Brother XII shipped her off to Switzerland to organize a foundation chapter. When she came back, he made it plain she was not wanted. She then moved to North Vancouver and disappeared from the record.

Brother XII was riding high again. As well as salting a fortune away, he was ruling an expanded empire. Mary Connolly bought De Courcy and Ruxton Islands, and gave them to the colony. He built a fine house for himself on De Courcy. But Mabel Skottowe was a sinister force. She renamed herself "Madame Z" and became the "enforcer" for the colony. Brother XII made himself more remote. Life for the colonists became much harsher. Madame Z would move people around from property to property, often for no obvious reason. People unused to physical labour were forced into back-breaking work. There was a break from this in 1930, when Brother XII and Madame Z went to England for a few months. But it started up again when they returned. Some of the behaviour was outright abusive.

It might be asked, why did people put up with such abuse? But these were people who had come to the colony because they trusted Brother XII. They sincerely believed he was working for their spiritual

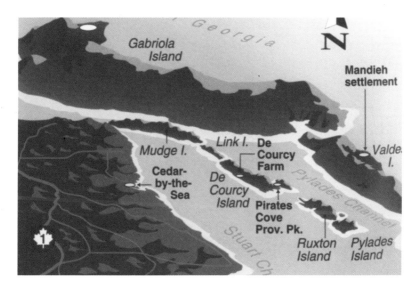

Map of Brother XII's settlements in BC.
COURTESY OF ROB STRUTHERS

good. Undoubtedly there was a strong element of denial in all this. Privately some were willing to admit that things had deteriorated. But people were also fearful. Brother XII and Madame Z had their spies in the colonists' midst and became aware of everything. Moreover, Brother XII had a reputation for practising black magic. People could not break the psychological grip he had on them.

The police were suspicious of this colony. They would occasionally land on the islands, under one pretext or another. In response Brother XII set up armed encampments. Camouflaged forts were constructed, where shots could be fired at approaching boats. He had all the colonists trained in firearm use. Finally the colonists began to rebel. They had a meeting and had Alfred Barley draw up a letter that was a "declaration of independence." When Brother XII received it, he was outraged. He tried to make separate deals with certain colonists. But he was wily enough to know the game was up. Sometime during June of 1932, Brother XII and Madame Z disappeared. The colonists never saw them again.

The colonists began a court case against Brother XII, to retrieve their money. They were initially fearful of doing so, because of his reputation for black magic. But when the case got under way, he never showed up. Also gone were the jars of gold coins. He had escaped to eastern Canada, and then made his way to England. Eventually, in 1935, he went to Switzerland, supposedly for medical treatment. There it was announced that he had died. But few people believed it, then or now. Most saw it as a convenient escape, back to the obscurity he had come from. Certainly no one found his money. Years later a caretaker discovered a secret compartment in a building on De Courcy. Thinking he might have found the money, he reached in and pulled out a piece of paper. But no treasure was there. Instead Brother XII had scrawled an angry message: "For fools and traitors—nothing!"

Brother XII has remained a riddle. Was he originally sincere in his beliefs, but then corrupted by power? Or was he always simply a scoundrel? Too little is known of his background to really be sure. And many of the newspaper accounts of the colony were wildly inaccurate. But the visions and early writings seem authentic. He was, after all, an unknown middle-aged man at the time. He couldn't have guessed at later developments.

Once in power, though, he was able to make the most of it. He had a gift for organizing and manipulating people. But the ends he put them to soon lost any spiritual reality. He was more than susceptible to the temptations of money, sex, and power. Once on the descent, he was vulnerable to a woman like Madame Z. So the enterprise collapsed and he was on the run. Many had originally seen him as a prophet or seer. For them it was a sad and bitter end.

Brother XII wanted to leave his mark on the world, and he did. His story shines a light on alternative communities in BC and the important part they played in its history. However, this is not a legacy he would have cared for. He was concerned with his spiritual message, not regions or countries. But his spiritual dreams are gone. Instead there is a province, the history of which he is now a part.

The Yuquot Whalers' Shrine in 1903. Photograph by George Hunt.

The Yuquot
Whalers' Shrine

IN THE EARLY 1990S SEVERAL groups of Mowachaht elders left their homes on Vancouver Island and travelled to New York. They had been invited by the American Museum of Natural History to see a mysterious object that had left their community ninety years ago. This object, the Yuquot Whalers' Shrine, is composed of an original small building and its contents: 88 carved human figures, 4 carved whales, and 16 human skulls. It was collected in 1904 by George Hunt, acting on the instructions of a museum curator, Franz Boas. The shrine had been built over several generations by Mowachaht ancestors, but few living band members had seen it. The question hanging over the elders was this: should the shrine come back home? But an outsider might well ask another question: why is it in New York at all?

Strange as its presence might seem in New York, it is in fact far from unusual. The American Museum of Natural History has an enormous northwest Native art collection, the largest in the world. And New York is not alone. Museums throughout the world have substantial collections of this art. So the shrine is part of a huge transfer of art and artifacts, from the Pacific Northwest to the rest of the world. The question really is, why did this transfer occur? In their original home, the art and artifacts had meaning and relevance. To the rest of the world, they did not. To understand why this happened requires examining the eighteenth century, when the first contacts between Native people and Europeans occurred in the Pacific Northwest. Only by studying their relationship, and its subsequent developments, can the answer be found.

Europeans were late arriving in the Pacific Northwest. In 1774, nearly three centuries after Columbus, the first Europeans sailed up the coast. Commanded by Juan Perez, they were exploring for Spain. They skirted Nootka Sound and the Queen Charlotte Islands, and were the first to contact Native people. From the very first they encountered people eager to trade. The Native people would paddle out to the ship, greet the Europeans, and almost immediately start to bargain. More than one European noted how adept they were at commerce. They were very anxious to acquire European goods, especially anything made of iron. In return they offered a wide range of items, such as carvings, ornamented blankets, and other objects of their own manufacture. Their most prized offering, though, was not something they had made. It was sea otter pelts, worth a fortune in China.

Four years after Perez, Captain Cook had the same experience. Sailing for Britain, he arrived at Nootka Sound in 1778. He stayed for nearly a month, which gave him plenty of time to buy goods and observe the Native people as traders. He noted that nothing seemed sacred, and that even their "gods" were for sale. But other officers noticed a difference. Some masks were sold furtively, which suggested "an impious crime." Other actions were more mysterious. When the Nuu-chah-nulth (Nootka) boarded Cook's ship, for example, they brought unusual carved heads. They simply gave these to the British, on condition they be displayed prominently. No one knows why.

Besides Native artifacts, Cook and his crew collected sea otter pelts and later sold them in China for a fabulous price. When this became known, other ships set sail for the region. These "sealers," as they were called, were soon making tremendous profits from the fur trade. The Native people were necessary partners, so some of this wealth flowed into Native hands. As a way of displaying this wealth, the Native elites commissioned more art.

Another factor spurred more art. As disease ravaged the Native communities, their population was drastically reduced. This compelled different tribal groups to band together in new communities. Since there was no status or "pecking order" in these communities, many were compelled to commission new poles, masks, and other artifacts. Ownership of such things was a time-honoured way of establishing rank. Moreover, the production of these items was now much easier. The artists were now able to use metal rather than stone implements.

This led to a "golden age" of northwest Native art. The famous nineteenth-century photographs show the result of this—villages with a forest of totem poles. But it also led to a tremendous surplus of goods. With the number of Native people continuing to dwindle, however, they were soon too few to use all the ceremonial gear. The missionaries also had an effect on the Native people: as they were converted to Christianity, the missionaries no longer tolerated their owning such property. The churchmen considered the masks, poles, and so on to be "heathenish" and compelled the converts to abandon them. The stage was set for a mass disposal of goods.

European collection of Native artifacts was, until the mid-nineteenth century, mostly sporadic. These artifacts were not seen as

George Hunt.

art, but in demand more as fascinating curios. In the late 1850s this started to change. A young curator at the Smithsonian, Spencer Baird, was becoming aware of the value of collecting these artifacts. He and some others were beginning to see that Native cultures were disappearing, and much more needed to be known about them. Moreover, the physical evidence of their cultures, their art and artifacts, would disintegrate if not collected by institutions. The great era of museum collecting was beginning.

A man living in the Pacific Northwest, James Swan, had been sending natural history specimens to the Smithsonian. He was close to the Native people and ideally placed to collect Native material. He asked the Smithsonian to do this, and Baird took him up on it.

Beginning in the 1860s, Swan began sending them items. They were particularly aimed at the Philadelphia Centennial Exhibition of 1876. Swan did a fine job, assembling over five hundred items, including a large canoe. The exhibit was a great success. In the 1880s he was sent up the coast again. Baird particularly wanted more collecting done, as foreign collectors were appearing on the scene. He was very worried that important material would disappear into European hands.

Baird was right to be concerned. The Germans were doing some major collecting. The biggest threat came from the Museum für Völkerkunde (Museum of Ethnology) in Berlin. There the director of the museum, Adolf Bastian, had hired a man named Adrian Jacobsen. Jacobsen was a seasoned collector and exceptionally able at his job. He acquired over two thousand items of very high quality, which covered the cultures comprehensively. If he had continued at this rate, little would have been left.

Luckily for Baird the Germans moved on. But one young German watched all this with interest. Franz Boas had been hired by Adolf Bastian to process the new material. He was a geographer but had become interested in anthropology. He had spent a year with the Inuit (known to Boas as Eskimo) on Baffin Island. Working with this material attracted him to another part of North America. His interest became even stronger when a troupe of Bella Coola dancers came to Berlin. He spent many hours with them and began learning their language. He developed a longing to go to the northwest coast and study the people and their culture.

Boas, in fact, wanted to leave Germany altogether. He found the intellectual life in Germany stultifying, and particularly disliked the anti-Semitism to which he was sometimes subjected. As well, he had a fiancée in New York. So he developed a plan to become a specialist on northwest coast culture, in the hopes of getting a job in New

York. In 1886 he got his chance to go to the northwest coast. He arrived in Victoria in September 1886 and spent the autumn visiting Native villages. He learned a great deal and collected many artifacts. When he left the coast, he went to New York, where he tried to get a job at the American Museum of Natural History. He had no luck, but did get a job as an editor at *Science* magazine. Now that he had a job, he married his fiancée and settled in the United States.

Before he left for the northwest coast, Boas had met Frederic Ward Putnam, the most prominent American anthropologist. Putnam was strongly impressed with Boas and knew he should be working for the American Museum of Natural History. When the museum hired Putnam as head of anthropology, he was determined to hire Boas. Putnam was successful, and in 1895 Boas joined the staff.

Boas knew that the museum's collection of northwest material was weak. The Smithsonian was no longer actively collecting in this field, but a major new competitor had emerged in the Field Museum of Chicago. Its new director, George Dorsey, was determined to acquire all the northwest material he could get. Boas had to act and so developed a bold new plan for his museum. He decided that a major anthropological expedition to northwest North America and northeast Siberia was needed. The idea was to send many scientists into the field over a six- or seven-year period. Boas would pick the people and direct their research. This would powerfully advance scholarship on the region. He managed to persuade the president of the museum, Morris Jesup, of the project's value. Jesup agreed and raised the money for it. In his honour it was named the Jesup North Pacific Expedition.

A major part of this expedition was to collect exhaustively among the northwest Native people. Boas wanted both artifacts and information. He needed the right person, and luckily he found him. On a trip to the northwest coast in 1888 Boas had met a Kwakwaka'wakw (Kwakiutl) man, George Hunt. The son of a Scottish trader and a Tlingit noblewoman, Hunt had grown up in the village of Fort Rupert. He was a full member of the Kwakwaka'wakw community and had insider access to information. He was also bilingual and had the intellect to prepare reports. He had worked with other collectors, most notably Adrian Jacobsen, and so could anticipate some of Boas's requests. Boas could not have found a better helper.

After some initial ethnographic training, Hunt got to work, and over the next few years he more than proved his worth. A large number of excellent items streamed into New York. This included some of the museum's most exceptional acquisitions. Occasionally Hunt understood an object's value better than Boas. The Dzonokwa bowl, for example, was a large and very expensive serving dish used at feasts. When Boas complained of its cost, Hunt wrote to him of its importance. He said that if he and Boas were to describe its use, the world would understand its value. Hunt became an important writer for the museum. He collected many texts, which were published under his and Boas's names. Occasionally Boas criticized Hunt's slowness, but Boas had to be wary, as other people knew Hunt's worth. George Dorsey of the Field Museum was always trying to inveigle him to leave. On occasion Boas had to warn Hunt not to talk to Dorsey.

In his ethnographic work, Boas had concentrated on the Kwakwaka'wakw. He saw them as the dominant culture of the region and the Nuu-chah-nulth as a pale shadow. So he told Hunt not to bother with the Nuu-chah-nulth. But Hunt took a trip to Nootka Sound in 1901. He told Boas of excellent collecting opportunities there. Boas knew he had to collect from all cultures, so he agreed to Hunt's trips, but they were far down Boas's list of priorities.

The Yuquot Whalers' Shrine in 1904. Photograph by George Hunt.
AMERICAN MUSEUM OF NATURAL HISTORY NEG. 104479

Hunt, though, became more interested. Talking with some Nuu-chah-nulth in 1902, he heard about a whalers' shrine. Intrigued, he travelled the next year to see it. But he was rebuffed. The Nuu-chah-nulth owners insisted on proper spiritual credentials. Hunt said he was a shaman and proved it by curing a man. So the owners gave him access. With the time available he took one quick photograph.

That photograph changed everything. Boas was fascinated, and it is easy to see why. Even today it is a powerfully haunting picture. In the photograph, the view is partially blocked by bushes. Beyond, dimly lit, is a wooden shed. A few rays of sun brighten the scene. Rows of strange, human-like figures line the shed. These figures have no arms, and all have different expressions. At their feet is a row of skulls. A larger skull, on the right side, is shining in mid-air. A few of the figures, caught by the sun, shine out of the gloom. The whole scene is utterly strange and mysterious. It was like nothing Boas had ever seen.

Adding to the mystery is the secrecy that has always surrounded the shrine. Hunt recorded some information in 1904, but it took him nearly twenty years to find more. The problem was that few tribe members knew very much. And when they did, they were unwilling to talk. The shrine was the property of the chief whaler, and only he could use it. Other tribe members were not even supposed to mention its existence. So Hunt could find few good informants.

What he did discover was that it was used in purification ceremonies before a hunt. The whaler needed to remove his scent, and absorb the power of his ancestors. One ritual, for example, involved strapping the mummy of his father to his back, then clutching a carved whale and plunging into a nearby lake. Another was beating his skin raw with branches, then plunging again into the lake. The whaler would spend several days in the shrine. The skulls and the human-like figures undoubtedly added to its power.

Boas knew he must have this shrine. A note of insistence crept into his letters, as he urged Hunt to get it. But Hunt was facing trouble. By 1904 he had much easier access to the shrine. Now, though, two people were claiming ownership, and each insisted he had the exclusive right to sell. Hunt was able to bring these two together and strike a deal. Even so, the shrine could not be taken from the community immediately. The owners said it must stay until the tribe departed for the sealing season. They feared an angry backlash.

By the end of 1904, the shrine had been dismantled and shipped to New York. Hunt was well pleased. In his letter to Boas, Hunt said,

"It was the best thing I ever bought from the Indians." But it proved a strange victory. It really marked a turning point in northwest collecting. A few months later Boas resigned from the American Museum of Natural History. He became a full-time university professor and left the museum world entirely. With Boas's departure, Hunt became far less active as a collector. He had some clients but became more involved in other projects. Dorsey left the Field Museum in 1906, and the whole market declined drastically. It carried on for some years, but essentially petered out by the 1930s.

The shrine disappeared from view after its arrival in New York. It was Boas's project, and with him gone no one cared to make a display of it. A few pieces have been exhibited over the years, but most have been in storage for a century.

Meanwhile, the fortunes of Native people have been reviving in Canada. Since the 1960s their sense of pride and self-worth has been escalating. The various tribal groups have become determined to recapture their cultural heritage. This of course includes the Mowachaht people, the heirs to the Whalers' Shrine.

In 1983 the Mowachaht began to consider a cultural centre, one that would include the Whalers' Shrine. Museums were coming under pressure to return art and artifacts to their original Native owners. In 1990 two other communities, Alert Bay and Cape Mudge, had their artifacts returned. With this in mind, the Mowachaht elders set off for New York.

Seeing the shrine was a powerful experience for them but left them divided. There were those who said it should come home, that it would revitalize the community. Others were not so sure. One said, "I don't want to see it on display—it's just too sacred." Another said, "You don't tamper with things you don't understand . . . you don't tamper with the Whalers' Shrine." For them the power still held.

George Hunt (the man on the left) is standing in front of a housepost in Fort Rupert.
IMAGE AA-00051 COURTESY OF ROYAL BC MUSEUM, BC ARCHIVES

The band as a whole, though, came to a decision. In November 1996 the band voted to formally request the return of the Whalers' Shrine and also began planning a cultural centre at Yuquot, where the history of the shrine and the band could be told. Here things have temporarily stalled. But the momentum is there, and one day the centre will be built.

The only remaining question is, will the shrine ever be open to the public? That would have been unthinkable in the nineteenth century. But as times change so does the meaning of the shrine. Once it was restricted to the chief whaler. Now all band members may see it, and in the future other people may be able to as well. When the band comes to make a decision, it will know what to do. The shrine will help them as it always has. It will guide the way.

The Royal Marine Camp on San Juan Island. The ship is HMS *Boxer*, which brought supplies from Victoria.
SAN JUAN ISLAND NATIONAL HISTORICAL PARK. PAINTING BY RICHARD SCHLECHT

The Pig War

THE LAST THING a person standing on the Oak Bay waterfront would think of is war. Beyond is an expanse of sea and sky, with the San Juan Islands off in the distance. Small boats bob in the water, and the occasional freighter glides by. It is a scene of peace and tranquility, far removed from the conflicts of the world. But war almost did erupt here. Britain and the United States nearly came to blows over the San Juan Islands. And the immediate cause was a runaway pig.

The origin of this dispute lay in the early nineteenth century. The Hudson's Bay Company had pushed west in its search for furs and established its headquarters on the lower Columbia River. By 1810 the British had a claim on the "Oregon territory," which was all the land west of the Rockies between the latitudes of 42° and 54°40'. But American settlers were moving into the southern Oregon territory. The Hudson's Bay Company knew it would not be able to hold on to this region for long, so the company sent an employee, James Douglas, up the coast to scout for a new headquarters. He found an ideal spot on southern Vancouver Island, and in 1843 Fort Victoria was established.

Three years later the British and American governments came to an agreement over the Oregon territory. By the Oregon Treaty of 1846, the boundary between British and American territory was to be the forty-ninth parallel west of the Rockies. When it hit water, it would go to the middle of the main channel between the mainland and Vancouver Island, then plunge south and follow the middle line out through the Strait of Juan de Fuca. But unfortunately the negotiators did not know their geography. There were two main channels between Vancouver Island and the mainland: Haro Strait and Rosario Strait. Between them lay the San Juan Islands. Until one channel was chosen the islands were up for grabs.

For several years it didn't matter. Settlement was so sparse that the border was of little concern. Things changed in 1853, when the company established a sheep farm on San Juan Island and sent thirteen hundred sheep there, under the care of Charles John Griffin. This alerted the local American customs officers. They demanded Griffin pay a duty on the sheep. When Griffin ignored them, they confiscated some of the sheep. James Douglas, governor of Vancouver Island, wrote to Governor Stevens of Washington Territory, bitterly protesting this action. Stevens in turn wrote to the US State Department asking for direction. The State Department said in effect to do nothing until a formal settlement was made. And there matters lay for the next few years.

In 1856 the British and American governments appointed negotiators to determine the boundary. But even as they got to work, the situation began to change. Gold was discovered in the Fraser River, and American miners poured into British Columbia. Some, not finding gold, decided to settle instead. To accommodate them American surveyors arrived on San Juan Island and began laying out farmsteads.

US general William Selbey Harney, the real instigator of the Pig War.
BRADY & CO., 1890

Early map of San Juan Islands and surrounding area.
PART OF A MAP BY GEORGE VANCOUVER, IN THE ATLAS VOLUME
OF *GEORGE VANCOUVER, A VOYAGE OF DISCOVERY...*, *1798*

This of course increased tension about the boundary and made some sort of incident inevitable. The spark for the hostilities was a runaway pig. An American, Lyman Cutler, had settled on one of the farmsteads. He was growing crops right beside the company's farm, where its pigs were used to running wild. Cutler built a fence, but the pigs got in and started eating his crops. Cutler complained to Charles Griffin, who responded that the entire area belonged to the Hudson's Bay Company. Cutler replied that he had been assured this was American territory, and his farm had been laid out by an American surveyor. Griffin ignored this and continued to let the pigs run wild. On June 15, 1859, a pig broke into Cutler's place, and started rooting in his crops. Enraged, Cutler grabbed his rifle and shot the pig. He then told Griffin what he had done and offered ten dollars in compensation. Cutler also said he would shoot any other animals found in his garden. Griffin replied that this was a particularly valuable pig and worth more like one hundred dollars.

Griffin reported this incident to James Douglas, who sent his son-in-law, A.G. Dallas, to the island to investigate. Douglas also assured Griffin he had his full support. Gradually this dispute cooled down and for the next few weeks lay dormant. And then General William Harney arrived on the scene.

The key to this whole dispute, and why it erupted, is the strange personality of William Harney. Born in Tennessee in 1800, he had joined the US Army at seventeen, and served many years with distinction. By the time of the San Juan Island dispute, he had risen to the rank of brigadier-general. But his judgment was often questionable. He had in the past ordered operations that were risky to the point of recklessness. Once, for example, he had invaded Mexico on his own initiative and had been cut off by Mexican troops. In the ensuing debacle, he had lost several men and his entire pack train. But such incidents did not deter him. If he thought he was right, he did what he wanted. He disobeyed the orders of one superior, General Winfield Scott. Only political connections saved him from court martial. But although Harney could be disobedient, he demanded absolute obedience from his own subordinates. He was appointed head of the US Army's Columbia District in 1858 and within months produced chaos in his office. Anything he deemed a slight was worthy of court martial. His superior, General Scott, tried to move him to another position, but Harney insisted on staying in the Pacific Northwest. And that, of course, made him commander of the San Juan Islands.

A few weeks after the pig incident, Harney made a tour of the islands. When he heard of the situation, he immediately sent 66 troops to San Juan Island. He picked as his commander a favourite of his, Captain George Pickett. Harney also declared American laws to be in force on the islands. This roused James Douglas, who sent three British warships to the island, commanded by Captain Geoffrey Hornby. Douglas also insisted that British laws prevail and picked a justice of the peace to enforce those laws. Pickett responded by appointing his own justice of the peace. The situation continued to escalate. Harney sent more troops, and they soon totalled 461. In response Douglas sent two more warships. There were now five British warships in front of the American camp, with a combined force of 2,140 men. A wrong move could have triggered an explosion.

The situation remained tense until early August. Then the British regional commander, Rear-Admiral R.L. Baynes, arrived. He realized at once this was a conflict they could not win. Due to the gold rush, BC's population at the time was mostly American. And with American forces to the south the British presence was simply not strong enough. On the American side, the American forces on San Juan Island had a new commander, Colonel Silas Casey. He warned Harney that British warship guns could destroy their camp. These men understood the dangers and kept a tight rein on their troops. No shots were fired.

In early September the British and American governments learned of this situation. Neither wanted war in this region. With a possible civil war looming, President Buchanan did not want any trouble with

The Royal Marines on San Juan Island in the early 1860s.
NATIONAL PARK SERVICE

the British government. He was most displeased with Harney's precipitous action. The British had many entanglements in Europe, and were not keen on war. Buchanan sent the head of the US Army, General Winfield Scott, to investigate. Knowing Harney as he did, he had a head start on the situation. After setting up headquarters in Port Townsend, Scott immediately began negotiations with James Douglas. Douglas, now that he was dealing with someone other than Harney, began to relax. He and Scott came to an agreement that each country would have a modest military presence on San Juan Island, until such time as the two countries could work out a formal settlement. There would be no more than one hundred troops for each country, which would keep each country's citizens safe and protect the island from marauding northern Native people. Scott informed Harney of this settlement and urged him to accept a transfer of duty.

Scott said the British, as a condition of a final settlement, would probably insist that Harney be relieved of his duty. Harney said that without a direct order he would not go.

Scott now left the region and went back to Washington. But before he left he put a small contingent of American troops on San Juan Island, under the command of Captain Lewis Hunt. With Scott out of the way, Harney saw his chance again. He ordered Lewis and his troops off the island and installed a company of his own under George Pickett. Harney then had Pickett turn over the government of San Juan Island to Washington Territory, and inform the British commander of the fact. He seemed determined to accomplish a de facto annexation.

But Harney had gone too far. The British commander informed Governor Douglas of what had happened, who in turn informed the British government. When the British told the American president, he was furious. On June 8, 1860, Harney was relieved of his command, ordered to report to Washington, and given a minor new post. When the Civil War broke out, he was given no further command. He retired in 1863.

The original agreement was now in force again. The British and the Americans set up camps at opposite ends of the island, with one hundred soldiers apiece. Relations from the start were very amicable. The two groups would have the occasional social or sporting event together. The officers, in particular, thoroughly enjoyed one another's company. Each group policed its own nationals, and each, when they caught a lawbreaker of the other nation, turned him over to that nation. This was of course a temporary situation, and nobody expected that it would last. But in the United States, the Civil War broke out in 1861 and lasted four years. After that came the years of

Reconstruction. Britain had many issues of its own. The San Juan Islands were not high on anyone's agenda. Eventually, though, the two countries realized they had to act. In 1872 they picked an independent arbitrator, the Kaiser of Germany, and asked him to make a binding decision as to what the "main channel" should be. The Kaiser referred the question to a panel of three academic experts. They decided two to one in favour of Haro Strait. The decision was accepted, and the boundary dispute was finally over.

On the island, people greeted the decision with mixed emotions. The military camps had been neglected, and many men were happy to be leaving. As well, there was often too little to do. But the troops had become part of the social fabric. An article in an American military journal even said, "Socially, our officers will regret the departure of their British associates, however they may rejoice at . . . our . . . title to the island." On November 21, 1872, the British flag was lowered for the last time. The original disputants were long gone, and their bellicose threats a distant memory. Common sense had prevailed, and the only victim had been the famous pig. The troops could sail away, secure in the knowledge that a dispute had been settled in the best possible way. But the British connection was gone for good.

"The caneing in Conduit Street," a contemporary caricature
of Lord Camelford's attack on George Vancouver.

The Vancouver /
Camelford Affair

THE DATE WAS SEPTEMBER 21, 1796. Captain George
Vancouver and his brother Charles were walking up Conduit Street
in London. They were on their way to an urgent meeting with
Lord Loughborough, the Lord Chancellor of England. Captain
Vancouver had been abused and threatened by a member of the
House of Lords. Since the assailant was a peer, Vancouver needed
help from the Lord Chancellor himself.

Suddenly a young man came dashing across the street, and attacked
the brothers with his cane. They fought back, and some onlookers
intervened, separating the men. The young man continued to utter
threats as he was pulled away.

The assailant was one Lord Camelford (Thomas Pitt), who had
recently inherited a seat in the House of Lords.

This strange event had its roots in the early lives of Thomas Pitt and
George Vancouver. Thomas Pitt, the future Lord Camelford, was born
in 1775. His family was one of the wealthiest and most powerful in

Britain. His uncle, William Pitt, was prime minister from 1766 to 1768 and later became the Earl of Chatham. William's younger son, also named William Pitt, who was Thomas Pitt's cousin, was prime minister from 1783 to 1801 and from 1804 to 1806. Other relatives also held positions of power. Thomas Pitt's father was not as prominent politically but was a very rich man. The family was a force to be reckoned with.

An elevated social status, though, did not lead to happiness for young Thomas. His family virtually abandoned him, and he grew up on a lonely Cornish estate. At age 11 he was sent to a school in Switzerland, where a kind headmaster gave him three happy years. Then at 14 he was sent to Charterhouse School, from which he soon ran away. He had had enough of school and wanted a naval career.

With his father's permission he soon got that career. In 1789 he was appointed a midshipman on the sloop *Guardian*. This ship was taking a load of plants, passengers, and convicts to Australia.

Somewhere in the Indian Ocean, the *Guardian* hit a giant iceberg. Many fled the ship, but some, including Pitt and the captain, remained on board. Eventually they managed to bring the crippled vessel back to Capetown. Pitt returned to Britain, a hero in the eyes of his family.

The iceberg incident only whetted Pitt's taste for adventure. He learned that an expedition was being mounted to Nootka Sound on the northwest coast of North America; because of a dispute with Spain, the government needed a negotiator there. At the same time, to reinforce the British presence on that coast, the government wanted a survey done by the Royal Navy from latitude 30° north to north of latitude 61° north (the northern limit of the Spanish claims of sovereignty). This survey would also determine whether there was a northwest passage. It was a major expedition. For an ambitious young midshipman like Pitt, this could be the trip of a lifetime.

The northwest coast of North America was probably the last major part of the continent that remained unexplored. Captain Cook's earlier voyages were renowned, but they had only begun to sketch the area. This trip was to be led by one of Cook's leading students, Captain George Vancouver. Pitt saw that it would be an enormous learning opportunity for him, and through his father's influence he secured a place on the ship.

Captain Vancouver was pleased. Meeting the young midshipman, he was convinced that Pitt had great potential as an officer.

George Vancouver was born in 1757, to a family of more modest means. His father had connections, though: he was deputy collector of customs in the town of King's Lynn. It was probably those connections that enabled Vancouver to sign on to Captain Cook's second expedition in 1772. Vancouver had been looking for a naval career. For someone who wanted to learn the trade, he couldn't have picked a better voyage. On Cook's ships the young seamen were given thorough training in seamanship and navigation. Vancouver was able and diligent, and Cook signed him on to his third voyage. They left England in 1776, settling sail on what was to be a pioneering exploration of the northwest coast of North America.

The main purpose of this voyage was to search for a northwest passage to Europe. None was discovered. The coastline was found to be long and complex; much surveying needed to be done if there was to be any hope of finding the passage in future expeditions.

Tragedy struck this voyage. In an altercation with the Sandwich (now Hawaiian) Islands natives, Captain Cook was murdered. Vancouver himself narrowly escaped death.

Vancouver's career continued to advance. He was promoted to the rank of lieutenant and spent most of the next decade in the West

Indies. In 1790 the decision was made to send an exploring expedition to the northwest coast. Vancouver was appointed captain in charge of the expedition's two ships, HMS *Discovery* and HMS *Chatham*.

Thomas Pitt was also on this expedition as an up-and-coming young midshipman. Initially Vancouver got along very well with Pitt. While the expedition was still in the South Atlantic, Vancouver even promoted Pitt to master's mate. The first sign of trouble occurred in Tahiti, where they anchored on December 27, 1791.

Tahiti was famous throughout the navy for its beautiful native women, who were generous with their favours. The men couldn't wait to get there. But Vancouver put the brakes on their ideas. He banned all contact with the Tahitian women, probably remembering the mutiny on the HMS *Bounty*, which had occurred a few years before. That mutiny had been attributed to the men becoming so infatuated with the local women that they were unwilling to resume their duties. Vancouver was determined to prevent this.

Not surprisingly, the decision was highly unpopular. Pitt, in particular, was not used to being denied his pleasures. One day, while on board the ship, he spotted a young lady nearby. Knowing how much the Tahitians wanted iron, he tossed her a barrel hoop in an attempt to win her favour.

But he was caught in the act. Vancouver had seen him and gave him twenty-four lashes for his disobedience—a harsh but not unusual punishment for the time. For Pitt it was a burning humiliation. Intensely proud of his aristocratic background, he could not bear the degradation of a common flogging. The seeds of revenge were sown.

Over the next three years of the expedition, Vancouver and his crew worked relentlessly to survey the complex mainland coast. Up to the Strait of Juan de Fuca the job was deceptively easy, but once they hit the mazes of Puget Sound the difficulties began.

Thomas Pitt, Lord Camelford, in a caricature from 1805.

Vancouver was respected by his crew, and they were willing to work hard for him. He was not well liked, though, especially by the young midshipmen. Vancouver was a stern disciplinarian; he was not unusually harsh, but the young midshipmen were often from the upper class and not used to the strict life of the navy. This was especially true of Thomas Pitt.

Vancouver gave Pitt more fuel for his resentment. Documentation is scanty, but it seems there were at least two more occasions when Pitt was whipped. During the first survey season, he was horsing around with his shipmates and broke the binnacle glass for the compass, for which he received his second flogging. The reason for the third flogging is not known, though it may have been linked to a skirmish Vancouver had with some Native people of the northwest coast. It was after this episode that Vancouver stripped Pitt of his rank as master's mate. Vancouver also named the place where the skirmish took place "Traitor's Cove." It is only possible to speculate, but perhaps this referred to some malfeasance of Pitt's on this site.

A final incident occurred at the end of the second survey season. Vancouver caught Pitt sleeping on deck, when he was supposed to be on duty. Pitt was locked in chains for two weeks and then completely released from duty. He was put onto the supply ship *Daedalus*, sailing to Port Jackson, Australia. From there he would have to make his own way home. Vancouver was rid of him at last. Or so he thought.

In the fall of 1794 Vancouver finally finished his three-year survey. In his relentless drive to complete it, Vancouver had become very ill. The crew headed home, arriving back in London in September 1795. Sick and exhausted, Vancouver remembered the adulation Cook had received when he returned and had hoped for a measure of the same.

But he was in for a disappointment. Vancouver was courteously but coldly received, and was not offered any special favours. Even his back pay, for five and a half years at sea, was not forthcoming. In fact he wasn't paid until November 1797, and then not very generously.

In retrospect this is not very surprising. The government would have been well aware of Vancouver's dealings with Thomas Pitt. Since key members of the government were relatives of Pitt's, they were hardly inclined to help Vancouver. Perhaps politically naive, Vancouver hadn't foreseen that disciplining Pitt would set him (Vancouver) up for trouble when he returned home.

Nevertheless, whatever people thought of Vancouver, it was still in the Admiralty's interest to publish his journal because a good profit would be made from its sale. Vancouver began preparing the journal in the spring of 1796.

But soon all hell broke loose. In September 1796, Pitt (now Lord Camelford) returned to England. Still bent on vengeance, a month or two earlier Pitt had sent Vancouver a challenge to a duel. Vancouver had replied that he was not personally responsible for actions committed as part of his official duties. Camelford's complaint would have to be investigated by a naval board of inquiry, to which Vancouver was willing to submit. This enraged Camelford. He went to Vancouver's house and verbally attacked him. After this incident, Vancouver was frightened and unsure what to do.

Encouraged by his friends, Vancouver was reassured that his initial response had been right. However, he was also aware that attempting legal action against a peer would be difficult if not hopeless. So Vancouver again wrote to Camelford, reiterating his position. Vancouver had his brother Charles deliver the letter. For his efforts Charles Vancouver was verbally attacked and abused.

A map of Vancouver Island drawn by George Vancouver.

It now became obvious that Vancouver could get help only from the Lord Chancellor, Lord Loughborough, so Vancouver made an appointment to meet with him. Vancouver and his brother were walking up Conduit Street, on their way to the appointment, when Lord Camelford spotted them. He dashed across the street, and the previously mentioned fight ensued. The attack ended only when some passers-by managed to separate the men.

Vancouver recovered himself and attended his appointment with Lord Loughborough, who agreed that the rivalry could not continue and arranged a meeting with Camelford.

Camelford, calmer now, met with Loughborough. He had to respect a senior peer like Loughborough, and was willing to agree to a peace bond for one year. But in reality he wasn't through with Vancouver yet.

A few days later a cruel cartoon appeared in the newspaper. Titled "The Caneing in Conduit Street," it was a drawing of the encounter between Pitt and Vancouver. It portrayed Vancouver as a quivering coward, and had some written asides attacking his character. James Gillray, a friend of Camelford's, had done the drawing.

The cartoon was libelous and inaccurate, but it managed to turn Vancouver, who had accomplished nearly as much as Captain Cook, into a laughingstock in his own country. Since Vancouver was at this point a very sick man, it's a wonder that he survived the humiliation.

But survive he did, for another year and a half, as he continued to work on his journal. He knew better than anyone else that it would be his vindication. Camelford continued to cause some trouble, but the worst was over. Vancouver almost finished the journal before died in May 1798.

Vancouver's brother John completed the journal, comprising three large volumes and a portfolio of maps, and it was published in the fall of 1798. It won instant acclaim and quickly sold out. Another edition was issued in 1801, and there were numerous foreign language editions. Vancouver is now recognized as one of the greatest explorers and map-makers of history, and his journal as a classic of exploration literature.

A less noble fate befell Lord Camelford. With much family assistance, he received the rank of lieutenant and the possibility of a naval career. But he was his own worst enemy. On October 25, 1797, he was commanding a ship near Grenada in the West Indies. He attacked, at night, what he thought was an enemy fort. It turned out to be an English fort, and he was fended off by its commander. A few days later he did something worse. In Barbados, he attempted to press some seamen into service. This was quite legal, since Britain was at war. However, such men often resist. When Camelford encountered resistance, he killed a seaman and a merchant captain. His family and his rank protected him from prosecution.

His bursts of violence got worse. He shot and killed a fellow officer who was not being sufficiently deferential. He horsewhipped a naval storekeeper who was slow at his job. Still his connections protected him. But the commanding officer of the West Indies fleet had had enough. Not wanting any more of his men killed or his forts attacked, he shipped his lordship home.

Over the next few years there was more wild and violent behaviour from Camelford. The press dubbed him the "half-mad lord." The end came in 1804. He had a quarrel with a friend over a high-class prostitute and challenged the friend to a duel. The friend came off best: he shot Camelford dead.

Camelford's defaming attacks on Vancouver had a lasting effect. Scholarship on Vancouver was affected by the bad press instigated by by his enemy. This could, perhaps, have been offset by access to Vancouver's personal papers, but unfortunately most of those have disappeared. The result has been an inadequate assessment of Vancouver's achievement. Only recently, especially thanks to the scholarship of W. Kaye Lamb, has this started to change.

Vancouver may not have been an easy person to work with. He was a demanding perfectionist, and the work of mapping the northwest coast was extremely difficult. But his men loyally respected him, and the historic mission was accomplished. Camelford, vengeful and malicious, wanted to keep Vancouver's story from being told. But he did not succeed. And it is Vancouver's name, not Camelford's, that is still prominent to this day.

The wedding party from the Curtis film.
EDWARD CURTIS

In the Land of
the Head Hunters

MOST PEOPLE IN CANADA AND the United States, whether they know it or not, have seen an Edward Curtis photograph.

Over more than thirty years, Curtis took thousands of pictures of Native North Americans. Best known for his portraits, he also depicted many scenes and traditions of the lives of Native people. A large selection went into his monumental work *The North American Indian*. In twenty volumes he provided full ethnographies of the tribes he dealt with, accompanied by the famous photographs. He devoted his life to this, hoping to preserve a vanishing way of life.

There was some urgency to his work. Like many of the educated elite of his time, he thought the Native North Americans were disappearing. As they disappeared, it was thought, so would the possibility of ever understanding their culture.

Living in Seattle in the 1890s, Curtis developed an interest in local Native people. It was a somewhat casual interest until an accidental meeting occurred. Curtis had become a mountaineer, and frequently climbed the local mountains. One day while climbing Mount Rainier, he happened upon several scientists who were stranded. They included Clinton Merriam, a founder of the National Geographic Society, and George Bird Grinnell, an expert on the Plains Indians. After rescuing them, Curtis showed them his photographic work. Impressed, they invited him to join the Harriman Alaska Expedition as official photographer.

This expedition was assembled in 1899 to study the physical and human aspects of the Alaska coastline. On it were some of the best-known scientists and natural history writers of the day. Curtis did very well and made many important connections. He became particularly good friends with Grinnell.

In 1900 Grinnell took Curtis to a sun dance ceremony in Montana. Curtis was stunned by what he saw. Thousands of Native people had gathered for several days of ceremonies. Curtis took many photographs of the Native people and began making friends with them. That visit changed Curtis's life. He knew he wanted to spend the rest of his life documenting the Native people of North America.

In the early 1900s Curtis began his work. He started with the Apache, Navaho, and other tribes of the American Southwest. The project, as Curtis envisaged it, would require a lot of money. His work was thorough and uncompromising. The ethnographic information, in both the writing and the photographs, had to be scrupulously exact.

Curtis did many months of fieldwork for every book in the series and paid assistants to help him. His standards for the end product were high: the books had to be of the finest materials and workmanship. As a result, Curtis was constantly fundraising. Luckily, he had friends in high places. President Roosevelt was a major supporter, and

Edward Curtis (self-portrait).

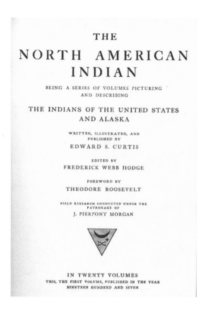

THE
NORTH AMERICAN INDIAN

BEING A SERIES OF VOLUMES PICTURING
AND DESCRIBING

THE INDIANS OF THE UNITED STATES
AND ALASKA

WRITTEN, ILLUSTRATED, AND
PUBLISHED BY
EDWARD S. CURTIS

EDITED BY
FREDERICK WEBB HODGE

FOREWORD BY
THEODORE ROOSEVELT

FIELD RESEARCH CONDUCTED UNDER THE
PATRONAGE OF
J. PIERPONT MORGAN

IN TWENTY VOLUMES
THIS, THE FIRST VOLUME, PUBLISHED IN THE YEAR
NINETEEN HUNDRED AND SEVEN

Curtis's book *The North American Indian.*
EDWARD CURTIS, 1907

the financier J.P. Morgan underwrote Curtis's production costs for the first few years.

The first two volumes of *The North American Indian* came off the press in 1907. They were hailed as masterpieces. Curtis, however, was heavily in debt. The money from Morgan could not cover all his costs, and other wealthy patrons were hard to find. He did manage to get more money from Morgan, but he knew he must find other sources.

Curtis began to go on lecture tours, giving early versions of slide shows to admiring audiences. Although a critical success, these shows did not make much money. But his next idea was brilliant.

Already, Curtis had experimented with the new medium of film to record aspects of Native life. He could also see that early versions of "Indian" films were very popular, despite being badly made. The idea came to him: why not combine the best of both? He could make a documentary film of true excellence and build it around an exciting plot. If badly made films could make a lot of money, what about ones that were of high quality? So new was this concept that no terms existed to describe it. Curtis called it a "documentary," but the concept of a documentary today would not usually include a fictional plot. "Docudrama" is perhaps closer.

Curtis began his work with the Kwakwaka'wakw (Kwakiutl) in 1910, when he had already completed nine of his projected twenty volumes. The Kwakwaka'wakw project had proved to be the most fertile of all. His photographs were known for their dramatic quality, and of all the North American tribes, the Kwakwaka'wakw had perhaps the richest and most dramatic ceremonial life. Moreover, they had preserved their old rituals more than any other northwest coast tribe had. So when the idea of a film came to Curtis, the Kwakwaka'wakw were the obvious choice as subject matter.

But to make the film as he wanted to, Curtis needed more than artistry. He needed someone from the Native community who could be his right-hand man.

He found him in George Hunt. The son of a Scottish trader and a Tlingit noblewoman, Hunt had grown up in the Kwakwaka'wakw town of Fort Rupert. He was a person of that culture but had a good command of English and understood European values. He had worked with several museum researchers, most notably Franz Boas from the American Museum of Natural History (see the tale "The Yuquot Whalers' Shrine"), so he could anticipate many of Curtis's needs.

There were, in particular, several things Hunt could do for Curtis. The first, and perhaps most valuable, was to be a source for

Kwakwaka'wakw (Kwakiutl) girl, circa 1914.
EDWARD CURTIS

ethnographic information. He was able, for example, to take Curtis to remote locations to see dances performed, dances that had been outlawed by the Canadian government. Many of these dances were later incorporated into the film, much to the delight of the Kwakwaka'wakw. Hunt knew all the cultural intricacies, such as who had the right to wear certain masks, and who had the right to work together. Without such guidance, Curtis could not have done his work.

Hunt was able to supply all the actors from the local community. His son, for example, was the male lead actor. Hunt provided all the necessary masks and props, and even carved one of the poles himself. His wife made all the traditional costumes. He found suitable locations for the film, locations that had no visible trace of white culture. And finally, of course, he could speak the local language, Kwak'wala. That meant he could direct the actors while Curtis ran the camera.

A great deal of what Hunt did is known by way of an account book he kept. Between October 1912 and October 1913, Hunt recorded all the items he acquired for the film, along with the date, purchase price, and who was being paid. For example, on December 24, 1912, he paid Mrs. George Hunt thirty dollars for twenty blankets she made. He also had a list of days worked by sixteen actors in April and May of 1914. Clearly, Hunt was important to the film, and an excellent record of its making exists.

Since the purpose of the film was partly to make money, the plot was pure melodrama. Onto the framework of a romance plot Curtis hung the true substance of the film, the documentary recordings. Numerous dances are featured, revealing how masks and other ceremonial objects were used.

Poster for Edward Curtis's film.
BILL UTLEY COLLECTION

Of the dances featured, the most spectacular one occurs in the war canoes. The scene begins with three large canoes approaching the village where a marriage is to take place. In the prow of each boat is a standing, costumed dancer, each representing a creature: Grizzly Bear, Thunderbird, and Wasp. As the canoes approach the shore, the dancers begin their dance. The dancing, the rhythm of the paddles on the water, and the strange, looming presence of the carved canoes are an extraordinary sight. Many people who have never seen the whole film have seen this clip.

Given its intentionally sensational title, *In the Land of the Head Hunters*, of course the film had to include some heads. Heads were indeed taken as war trophies, but that was the extent of the "head hunting"; it was not a part of Kwakwaka'wakw ceremonial life. This fact led to a title change when the film was first restored. The new title, *In the Land of the War Canoes*, better reflects the film's subject matter and the Kwakwaka'wakw way of life.

Curtis never lived to see the revival of his work, which happened decades after it had met with critical acclaim but financial failure. Desperately short of money, he sold all rights to the film in 1923. Despite many difficulties he managed to finish his great series, *The North American Indian*. In later years he worked in Hollywood but never made another film himself. He died in 1952.

Interviewed many years later, surviving Kwakwaka'wakw elders expressed pleasure at having worked with Curtis. He had enabled them to revive some traditional practices and bypass contemporary prohibitions against their ceremonies. His collaboration with the tribe had helped the younger members learn the old ways and take pride in their traditions.

INTERIOR OF A HABITATION IN NOOTKA SOUND.

John Jewitt

IN 1807, A SHORT BOOK, *A Journal Kept at Nootka Sound*, was published. It was the story of John Jewitt, a young sailor held captive by the Nuu-chah-nulth (Nootka).

It consisted mostly of short notes about his everyday life and had little literary merit. It received little notice and could well have disappeared. But scattered here and there were intriguing bits of information. They hinted at a fascinating story behind the narrative.

Jewitt's contemporary Richard Alsop certainly thought so. Alsop was one of the leading writers and public figures in New England. He and other writers were attempting to forge a new American literature, and were looking for new themes. Jewitt's book had possibilities.

Alsop therefore arranged to meet with Jewitt. Using the journal as his basis, Alsop conducted four long interviews with Jewitt. It was a difficult business. Jewitt, although very intelligent, was not much of a raconteur. But Alsop worked hard, and a fascinating story began to emerge.

Jewitt was born and grew up in England. He had been well educated but preferred to be a blacksmith. He was restless and had an itch to see the world. Living in the port town of Hull, he saw many ships come in. One day a ship bound for North America arrived. A blacksmith was needed, so he signed on board.

It was an "otter ship." These ships traded with the northwest tribes for sea otter pelts, and sold them for a fortune in China. Jewitt appears to have enjoyed his sojourn aboard. He liked and respected his captain, and seems to have gotten along well with the rest of the crew. The trip went relatively quickly, and after six months they arrived at Nootka Sound.

Nootka Sound was not their main destination. They stopped there to get fuel and supplies, and do a little trading with the local tribe. But what the white visitors didn't know was that trouble was brewing with the local Native people. Other otter ships had treated them badly, killing some and stealing their furs. Anger had been building up among the Nuu-chah-nulth and was on the verge of exploding. Normally otter ships were wary of allowing Native people on board, but Captain Salter did allow them, after first checking to make sure they had no weapons. The captain made a present of a musket to their chief, Maquinna. But when Maquinna took it home, it malfunctioned. He took it back to the captain, but Salter disparaged Maquinna, saying it was good and that Maquinna hadn't used it properly. This drove Maquinna into a murderous rage.

The next day, the Nuu-chah-nulth came back on board with smuggled weapons. At a prearranged signal they attacked, massacring almost the entire crew. Jewitt was saved because of his skills. Maquinna knew he could make very good weapons and other implements, and made him a slave. Later it was discovered that another European, John Thompson, had also escaped the massacre. Jewitt pleaded for Thompson's life, saying that Thompson was his father. It's unlikely that Maquinna was deceived, but he knew Thompson was a sail-maker and could be useful as well. So Maquinna spared him.

John R. Jewitt.

Jewitt and Thompson had to adapt to Native life. It was very difficult. They were despised by the tribe, and completely at Maquinna's mercy. The food was different and hard to eat. Medical attention was nonexistent. They lived in constant terror for their lives and had no conceivable means of escape.

But life did start to improve. Jewitt, in particular, adapted.

He made the weapons and tools his captors needed and went out of his way to make fine ornaments. He became a personal favourite of Maquinna. Jewitt began to integrate into the Native way of life. He adopted Native dress and was initiated into Nuu-chah-nulth rituals. When they moved to different camps, he went with them. Thompson was a different story. He never relented in his hatred of the Nuu-chah-nulth and would occasionally have fights. Jewitt was constantly interceding for him. But when he and Jewitt took part in a raid on another tribe, he killed seven of the enemy. After that the Nuu-chah-nulth let him alone.

One day a ship hove into view. Captain Hill and the brig *Lydia* caused great excitement in the village, but Jewitt pretended not to care. Maquinna, though, was anxious to go on board and asked Jewitt to write a letter of recommendation. This was Jewitt's chance. He wrote a letter blaming Maquinna for the massacre, and asked the captain to capture Maquinna and arrange an exchange. Jewitt felt safe doing this, because none of the Nuu-chah-nulth could read English. The tribe members suspected a trap and told Maquinna not to go. But Maquinna was so keen he ignored their advice. He was duly captured.

In due course the exchange was made, and Jewitt bade farewell to Maquinna. A strange bond had developed between them. They met again a few months later, when the *Lydia* returned to pick up furs. They greeted each other warmly, then they said goodbye forever.

After settling in Connecticut, Jewitt published his journal.

Sometime in the next few years, Richard Alsop read the journal and saw its potential. After interviewing Jewitt, he wrote a full book on Jewitt's adventures called *A Narrative of the Adventures and Sufferings, of John R. Jewitt; Only Survivor of the Crew of the Ship* Boston. He published it under Jewitt's name in 1815. Alsop apparently did not wish to claim any credit. It was an immediate bestseller and went through numerous printings. Many editions have been published in the two centuries since, and the book is still in print today.

It was an excellent example of a "captivity narrative"—stories of white people who had been captured by and forced to live with Native tribes. The book was a new and popular genre and distinctively North American. But the biggest reason for its popularity has to be the quality of the writing. Two centuries later, it is still an enjoyable book to read.

Alsop died soon after the publication of the book. Jewitt, though, benefited from its sales. He took to travelling the Eastern Seaboard peddling it. Later there were stage versions, in which he took part. Despite marrying and having a family, he still seemed to prefer the roving life. His letters home give some idea of his last years. He died in 1821.

Jewitt's *Narrative* works on several levels. First, and perhaps foremost, it is a classic work on West Coast Native ethnography. Jewitt was living with the Nuu-chah-nulth at a time when they were relatively untouched by white civilization. He records their everyday life, and the book is a particularly rich source of information about their material culture.

Second, it is an important document in the commercial history of the West Coast. After Cook and Vancouver, the main Western presence on the coast were the otter ships. Documents on this trade are scarce, as captains wanted to keep their sources secret.

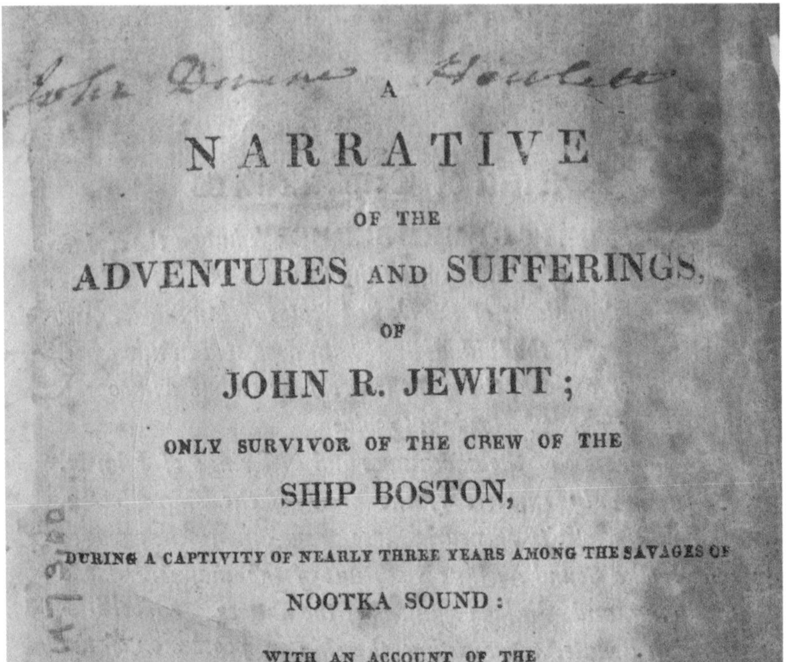

A

NARRATIVE

OF THE

ADVENTURES AND SUFFERINGS,

OF

JOHN R. JEWITT;

ONLY SURVIVOR OF THE CREW OF THE

SHIP BOSTON,

DURING A CAPTIVITY OF NEARLY THREE YEARS AMONG THE SAVAGES OF

NOOTKA SOUND:

WITH AN ACCOUNT OF THE

MANNERS, MODE OF LIVING, AND RELIGIOUS

OPINIONS OF THE NATIVES.

EMBELLISHED WITH A PLATE, REPRESENTING THE SHIP IN POSSESSION OF THE SAVAGES.

"Dire scenes of horror on a savage shore,
"In which, a witness sad, a part I bore."

Title page from the second edition of Jewitt's *Narrative*.
FROM THE COLLECTION OF THE GREATER VICTORIA PUBLIC LIBRARY

Third, it is an important text in the history of American literature. Alsop and his literary friends had been searching for ways to fuse classic literary styles with North American themes. The *Narrative* is a brilliant example of that. Its enormous popularity must have been gratifying proof that they were on the right track.

Last, and by no means least, is its role in West Coast literature. This is, after all, a story of BC and of the early themes in its history, particularly exploration, fur trading, and the relations between the Native people and Europeans. Jewitt illuminates all of these themes, and does so in a wonderfully readable way. The book is a highly recommended read for all British Columbians.

Victoria's second Christ Church Cathedral.

The Battle of
the Bishops

DISPUTES IN THE ANGLICAN CHURCH often tend to be quiet
affairs. Strongly held views on various topics certainly exist, but traditionally debates have mostly occurred in hushed tones over teacups.
This was definitely not the case in early Victoria, however.

Church membership was far more widespread than it is today,
and opinions on church life and conduct were part of everyday life.
So when the two most senior and respected clerics held different
views on the conduct of church services, there was bound to be
trouble. And in the early 1870s, trouble did erupt.

The man at the centre of this dispute was the Very Reverend
Edward Cridge, dean of Christ Church Cathedral. Cridge had come
to Victoria in 1855, in response to a request from the Hudson's Bay
Company. It needed a clergyman for its Pacific Northwest base, Fort
Victoria. Cridge and his wife, Mary, came and quickly became essen-
tial members of the community.

The Cridges wound up doing several jobs simultaneously.

The Rev. Edward Cridge and Mary (Mrs. Edward) Cridge.
IMAGE A-01205 COURTESY OF ROYAL BC MUSEUM, BC ARCHIVES
IMAGE A-01304 COURTESY OF ROYAL BC MUSEUM, BC ARCHIVES

Cridge was the only clergyman in the region and often had to go on rough roads as far as Colwood and Metchosin to minister. He also had a glebe (clergyman's allotment) of one hundred acres to clear and use to feed his family. As if that were not enough, he established the first hospital in 1858, and in 1860 became the new colonial government's inspector of schools. Mary Cridge, in addition to bearing and raising several children, helped him in all his social endeavours and was a driving force in establishing the British Columbia Protestant Orphans' Home in 1873 (now the Cridge Centre for the Family). They were the early colony's champions of the underprivileged and the unfortunate, and the leading force for social action.

The gold rush in the late 1850s caused a huge expansion in Victoria's population. Large numbers of transients travelled into and out of the region, and the political and social structures were unable to cope. Cridge appealed to Britain to send more clerical staff. In response, the Anglican Church appointed a new bishop for the colony, George Hills, who arrived in 1860. Having run the show up until then, Cridge now had to answer to a new boss.

At first all went well. The two men respected each other, and for the first few years everything was calm. But there was always an underlying tension between them.

Cridge was a low churchman, who liked plain services with an unadorned altar and wore black habit. Bishop Hills, on the other hand, was a son of the Oxford Movement—a neo-Catholic revival in the Church of England, which emphasized ritual and elaborate dress in its services. To a low churchman, such things could smack of "popery."

On December 5, 1872, there was a consecration service for the new Christ Church Cathedral. Archdeacon Reece came from Quamichan to preach. Reece, an appointee of Bishop Hills, was a high churchman. In this sermon he advocated more ritualism in the services. This was too much for Cridge. At the end of the service he got up and protested vehemently. The bishop could not ignore this breach of canon law. The men proceeded to exchange a series of heated letters.

This correspondence culminated in a letter Cridge wrote to the local newspaper. In this letter, published on January 9, 1874, he publicly repudiated the bishop's authority. In response, Bishop Hills brought Cridge before an ecclesiastical court. A trial was held, and when Cridge was found guilty, his licence was revoked.

George Hills, first Anglican bishop of BC.
IMAGE A-01365 COURTESY OF ROYAL BC MUSEUM, BC ARCHIVES

Cridge would not take this lying down. He demanded the case be brought before an unbiased, secular court. The case was then heard before Chief Justice Matthew Baillie Begbie. On October 24, 1874, Begbie found in favour of the bishop. He forbade Cridge to be rector of Christ Church Cathedral or to act as a clergyman for the Anglican Church.

Cridge accepted this verdict, but it tore the social fabric of Victoria apart. Many of the oldest and most prominent families were supporters of Cridge. When Cridge left the Anglican Church and joined the Reformed Episcopal, many churchgoers in Victoria followed him. Prominent among them was Sir James Douglas, who donated land at Humboldt and Blanshard streets for the new Church of Our Lord. Cridge became the rector of this new church and was soon a Reformed Episcopal bishop. He ministered to this new church until 1895 and continued to be active in social work thereafter. He died in 1913.

Cridge's legacy lives on, through the church he founded and in the Cridge Centre for the Family. Despite this, Cridge's life and work are now largely forgotten, except in the historical records.

A cartoon of John Gustavus Norris, Amor De Cosmos, and Mifflin
Wistar Gibbs created by Victoria confectioner Andrew W. Piper.

Mifflin Wistar Gibbs

ONE HUNDRED AND FIFTY YEARS ago, Victoria was a rough-and-ready frontier town, filled with Americans who had streamed north in 1858, looking for gold. The population ebbed and flowed as people travelled to and from the goldfields. It was a sometimes rowdy and unstable place.

One large group of Americans, though, stood out. A party of six hundred blacks had fled north from California to escape persecution. Governor Douglas had welcomed them, and assured them they would be treated with fairness and equality. The unofficial leader of this group was a prosperous San Francisco merchant, Mifflin Wistar Gibbs, who originally was from Philadelphia.

In a British colony, Gibbs was an unlikely pioneer. He had done well in his home country, and only racist persecution could have forced him to leave. Born into a "free" black family in 1823, he was largely self-educated. His family was poor, but he had managed to become a carpenter. His mother had insisted that he have a trade to fall back on.

Gibbs was intelligent and industrious, and prospered in his work. He also became politically active. He was involved with the

M. W. GIBBS.

Mifflin Wistar Gibbs, left. Peter Lester, Gibbs's business partner, right.
WILLIAM J. SIMMONS, 1887

Philadelphia "station" of the Underground Railway, which helped black slaves escape to Canada. He met and became friends with social reformer and abolitionist Frederick Douglass. Together, they toured western New York State, giving anti-slavery lectures.

Discouraged by a lack of opportunities at home, Gibbs headed west. It was 1850, the time of the California gold rush. He quickly found work as a carpenter and started saving money, eventually accumulating enough to go into business for himself. He formed a partnership with a man named Peter Lester, and they opened a shop selling boots and shoes. Their business flourished.

While blacks could prosper financially in California, they faced severe restrictions. California was admitted to the Union as a "free" state in 1850, but blacks were not allowed to vote or testify against whites in court. Fugitive slaves were not safe in California; they could be arrested and returned to their masters. By the late 1850s, the situation was becoming very difficult. Laws were proposed that would, in effect, reinstitute slavery.

Many blacks realized they must leave. In 1858, a "Pioneer Committee" of sixty-five sailed north to Vancouver Island, and three paid a visit to Governor Douglas, who assured them they would have full civic rights. For Douglas, their immigration was a blessing—he was afraid Vancouver Island would be overwhelmed by white Americans and Britain would lose the colony, as it had the Oregon Territory. Such an industrious, reliable group as these blacks not only would provide a good work force, but also would be a strong force against annexation.

In the spring and summer of 1858, the rest of the emigrating blacks moved north. It was a diverse group, ranging from the well-educated to the illiterate. Vancouver Island, though, needed workers at all levels, and soon, most of the black immigrants were fully employed. Gibbs did well—he had had the sense to bring a large supply of goods for miners. He sold them quickly and with the proceeds bought a building that he converted into a shoe store, where he was soon back in business with Peter Lester. Over the next few years, Gibbs acquired more investments and real estate. A year after he arrived, he met Maria Alexander, another American, from Oberlin, Ohio. The two married and had five children, all born in Victoria.

A year after the group arrived, a dispute, known as the Pig War, erupted between Britain and the United States over the San Juan Islands. Victoria was also vulnerable to raids from northern Native people. In response, with the governor's blessing, the all-black Victoria Pioneer Rifle Company was formed. Volunteers in this company built a drill hall that also became a community centre for black people.

Uniforms were ordered from England. The militia was mostly a self-supporting, although it received a bit of government money. One thing its members did not have was adequate weapons. They had to make do with flintlocks.

Despite the obvious value of the black immigrants to the community, prejudice began to show. While schools were integrated and only one church insisted on segregation, politics was a different story. One incident, in particular, fuelled the flames. An unscrupulous Attorney General, George Hunter Cary, wanted to secure political advantage in the colony's elections of 1860. He was a member of Douglas's party, which was seeking to defeat Amor De Cosmos in the Victoria riding. De Cosmos was editor of the *British Colonist* and a bitter opponent of Douglas and his "family compact."

Cary told the black community they were eligible to vote, despite having been on Vancouver Island little more than a year. Citing the Dred Scott decision in the United States Supreme Court, which found that no person of African ancestry could claim citizenship in the United States, he told them they could vote because they were not citizens of another country. He knew they would vote for Douglas's party.

The black people did vote and, as predicted, they favoured Douglas's party. Their votes were the decisive factor in defeating De Cosmos. De Cosmos erupted in fury. In his paper, he attacked the validity of the black vote.

That was fair comment, but in his anger De Cosmos did far more. He initiated a racist campaign that went on for years. He not only made vicious comments, but also purposely published anti-black stories. Gibbs, as the black community's unofficial spokesman, wrote to the paper complaining of this treatment. He emphasized that the black citizens were strong supporters of the British Constitution. But his voice of reason was not heard.

De Cosmos's behaviour undoubtedly contributed to a worsening of race relations. As well, people were affected by the prolonged Civil War to the south. Whatever the cause, blacks began to encounter more barriers. Some saloons, for example, would not allow them to enter. In theatres, they were often relegated to undesirable seats. A nasty incident occurred in 1861, when Gibbs and one of his black business partners went to the theatre for a benefit, and someone threw a bag of flour at them. A melee ensued, and the perpetrators were identified. Several white men were arrested and went on trial, but were acquitted because witnesses would not testify against them. De Cosmos's *British Colonist* refused to condemn the attack.

By 1864, anti-black prejudice had become widespread. That year, Douglas retired and Gibbs and Lester were denied tickets to the banquet in his honour. To his lasting shame, Douglas did nothing. Later, all blacks were barred from attending a banquet for the Queen's birthday.

Then there was a final insult. A parade was being organized to honour the new governor, Arthur Kennedy, and the Victoria Pioneer Rifle Company wanted to participate. As the first citizen militia in the city, it was an obvious choice. But the organizing committee rejected the company, saying it was afraid of how some members of the community would react.

The following year, though, the Civil War in the United States ended, and things began to change. Many Americans left Victoria, and much of the anti-black sentiment dissipated. Life became easier for the remaining black community. In November 1866, Gibbs ran for city council. He had tried before, in 1862, and lost. Now, however, he was elected. A measure of his acceptance, perhaps, is that he won in James Bay, the

Advertisement for Gibbs and Lester's business on Yates Street.
BRITISH COLONIST, JANUARY 31, 1860

wealthiest ward in the city. He was named finance chair on council and even served for a time as acting mayor.

A final political honour came in 1868, when Gibbs was elected as Salt Spring Island's representative to the Yale Convention. Established by Amor De Cosmos, the convention set British Columbia's terms for Confederation. As a measure of how far things had come, these two were now able to work together. It was a remarkable change.

Gibbs was a restless man, and in early 1869 he took on a new challenge. He invested in a coal mine in the Queen Charlotte Islands, and agreed to supervise the operations, relinquishing his seat on Victoria's city council. He supervised the mine for a year but soon grew dissatisfied. He returned to Victoria and relinquished his investments—the pull of his native country was too strong and he wanted to study law in Oberlin, Ohio. In 1870, he left Victoria for good.

The departure of Gibbs was a decisive change for the black

community. For more than a decade, he had been its leader. The number of black people declined as other groups grew. The Chinese community, in particular, was acquiring much more importance. But for blacks then, life was improving south of the border. The great need for a safe haven disappeared, and there had been no other comparable flood of black immigration north.

After leaving Victoria, Gibbs went on to an outstanding career. In 1873, he was elected a municipal judge in Little Rock, Arkansas, the first black American to be so elected.

After his judicial career, he served in important government posts, including as US Consul to Madagascar in 1897. He retired in 1901, at the age of 78, and died in 1915. Eight years before that, however, Gibbs paid a visit to Victoria. He returned to a vastly different city. Most people he knew from the past were dead, including his old foe-turned-friend, Amor De Cosmos. But De Cosmos's brother, C. McK. Smith, was still alive. Gibbs looked him up, and they discussed old times.

Gibbs's relations with De Cosmos, and perhaps with Smith, show why Gibbs was such an effective leader. He preferred to work with people rather than against them and to win opponents over by reason. But if people did attack him, he bore no grudges.

Gibbs had been a great leader of an important community. In his day, up to one-fifth of the population of Victoria was black. When the blacks arrived, Victoria was a fast-changing society with an unpredictable future. They played a major role in the community, providing stability and helping it thrive.

But their importance goes beyond that. They were the first large non-white group to arrive in Victoria and blend in with the community, and so were a successful example for others to follow.

Amor De Cosmos.

Amor De Cosmos

ONE DAY IN THE LOCAL History Room of the GVPL, I came across a book that seemed odd for the library's collection. Its title was *The New Municipal Manual for Upper Canada* and it was published in 1859. What could be the reason for its presence here? Then, as I started to put it back on the shelf, I noticed a mark on its outer pages—a stamp with a person's name, "A. De Cosmos." Looking inside, I saw the title page had a matching signature, "A. De Cosmos." The mystery was solved. Amor De Cosmos had owned the book.

Amor De Cosmos is one of the major founding fathers of British Columbia, one of the least known, which is strange because his achievements are beyond dispute. Arriving in Victoria in 1858, he established Victoria's first newspaper, the *British Colonist*. He began agitating for more democratic government and in his editorials relentlessly attacked the colonial government of Sir James Douglas. De Cosmos's aim was to end the rule of a privileged elite.

This inevitably led him into politics. Leaving the paper in 1863, De Cosmos embarked on a political career. Starting off as Victoria's representative in the Vancouver Island House of Assembly, he rose

CHANGED HIS NAME

An Eccentric Character Now Lying at Death's Door in Victoria.

SMITH TO DE COSMOS

His Remarkable Performance With a Tough Beefsteak a at Kalama Hotel.--Member Parliament.

The Hon. Amor de Cosmos, one of the first members British Columbia sent to the Dominion parliament, is very ill at his home in Victoria. The forty-niners of California will best recall him under the name of John Smith, an American, who was something of a globe-trotter.

An article about Amor De Cosmos.
THE SPOKESMAN-REVIEW, DECEMBER 15, 1895

to become BC's second premier (1872–1874) and Victoria's MP in the federal House of Commons (1871–1882). He had three major triumphs in his career. One was a successful lobbying effort to have a railway built linking the province to the rest of Canada. His only regret was that it ended in Vancouver, not Victoria. Second, he led the push for BC to join Confederation. This occurred in 1871. Finally, as premier he did not invite the Lieutenant-Governor (as had previously been customary) to sit in on Cabinet meetings. This ensured the political supremacy of the elected legislature in the province.

Why, then, is De Cosmos so little known today? His choice of a name may have something to do with it. Born William Alexander Smith, he changed his name to Amor De Cosmos during the California gold rush. Apparently he wished to lose a common name and acquire a more exotic one. Doing so had the effect, though, of making him look slightly ridiculous to succeeding generations. Another reason for his obscurity was his disputatious personality. In the early stages of his career, his combative personality helped achieve necessary political reform, but in later years, his personality deteriorated, and he became odd and reclusive. In 1895 De Cosmos was declared "of unsound mind," and he died two years later. Only a handful of people came to his funeral.

No. 6 coal mine, Cumberland, BC.
IMAGE B-07607 COURTESY OF ROYAL BC MUSEUM, BC ARCHIVES

Ginger Goodwin

DRIVING INTO COURTENAY ONE DAY in the late 1990s, I saw a sign on the highway that said, "Ginger Goodwin Way."

Goodwin, I knew, had been a labour leader in the early twentieth century and a strong socialist. During the First World War, he had preached pacifism. He antagonized many with his labour organizing and opposition to the war. He was shot and killed by the police, supposedly because he was a war evader. His being commemorated by a sign seemed strange to me.

People in the labour movement, though, considered Goodwin to be a hero. The real reason for his death, they said, was that he was such an effective labour organizer. To many, he was—and is—a martyr to progressive causes.

Goodwin was obviously far more controversial than the sign would indicate. But feelings seemed to have mellowed, and he was finally getting his due. Appearances, though, were deceiving. In 2001 the provincial government changed from a pro-labour to a pro-business party. A few months later, the sign was gone.

Who was this man who still aroused such controversy?

Albert (Ginger) Goodwin was born in England in 1887. His father was a coal miner in Yorkshire, and young Albert joined him in the pits at age fifteen. It was a hard and dangerous life. Accidents were frequent, and there was always the possibility of cave-ins.

Life was little better out of the pits. Housing and sanitation were bad, and there were frequent outbreaks of typhoid. No wonder Goodwin left England when he was nineteen and sailed to Canada.

When Goodwin arrived in Glace Bay, Nova Scotia, he would have found conditions little improved from back home. The rapidly expanding population had outstripped the housing supply, resulting in poor water and sanitation. The men worked long days, often ten or more hours. The United Mine Workers of America (UMWA) was attempting to organize the workers, but the employer refused to recognize the union.

The employer would negotiate only with the Provincial Workmen's Association, which was little better than a company union. The result was, as one writer put it, "one of the longest and most bitter strikes in Canadian history." It ended in a complete defeat for the union, and a blacklisting of those who had participated in the strike. Goodwin and others were forced to move west to look for work.

In coming to BC, Goodwin was encountering some of the most dangerous mines in the world. The mine owners were particularly lax about gas and coal dust. The result was several major explosions that killed hundreds of miners in the late nineteenth and early twentieth centuries. No wonder the miners began expressing interest in the UMWA. But they had to deal with owners like James Dunsmuir, a vehement opponent of unions.

Goodwin came to work in the mines of Cumberland on Vancouver Island. As in Nova Scotia, tensions were building between the coal

"Ginger" Goodwin

Ginger Goodwin.

miners and their employers. The workers complained of poor pay and unsafe working conditions. The mine owners seldom listened, secure in the knowledge that the provincial government was mostly on their side.

The few regulations about mine safety were frequently ignored. In response, the miners invited the UMWA to the Comox Valley in 1911. Then a worker was fired—the union said for reporting gas in mines. The workers walked off the job on September 16, 1912. The strike did not end until almost two years later, on August 20, 1914.

Vancouver Island's Great Coal Strike, as it came to be known, was long and bitter. The companies hired strike-breakers, and soon, the mines were producing again.

The companies, with the exception of the Jingle Pot mine in Nanaimo, refused to recognize the union. Jingle Pot mine signed a contract with the UMWA in August 1913, and the men there returned to work. The workers at the other mines grew increasingly desperate and frustrated. Riots broke out that month in Ladysmith, Extension, and Nanaimo. In response, the provincial government brought in the militia. Many men were arrested. The strike ground on for another year before the union was forced to call a halt. It was financially ruined.

The miners were defeated. The companies refused to recognize the union and imposed a settlement the miners had to accept. The strikers were blacklisted and had to look for work elsewhere.

Goodwin had to leave Cumberland to find work. After two short mining jobs in the Interior, he got a job as a smelterman in Trail. The Socialist Party of Canada picked him as its local candidate in the 1916 provincial election. He had become a very good public speaker and ran a vigorous campaign. He didn't win but made a respectable showing. In the wake of the election, he slowly rose through the union ranks, and by early 1917 was elected by the BC Federation of Labour as its vice-president for the Kootenay District.

Under Goodwin as president, the union started moving toward a strike. The main issue was hours of work. The union wanted eight-hour days for all members of the smelter workforce. The company insisted it had an agreement allowing longer hours. On November 15, 1917, the smeltermen walked off the job. By December, however, they were back, after mediators determined there was an agreement in place for the duration of the war, and urged the men to return and lobby for legislated eight-hour days.

Goodwin, meanwhile, was having trouble with the government. Years of working in mines had made him a chronically sick man. When conscription began in 1917, Goodwin was medically examined and determined to be temporarily unfit, but subject to re-examination later. Eleven days into the strike, he received a telegram ordering him back for re-examination, at which he was declared fit for fighting. The union denounced this as highly suspicious.

Determined not to fight, Goodwin fled to the wilds west of Cumberland. Conscription was massively unpopular in Canada, and Goodwin had company in the bush.

Several other men were also holed up west of Comox Lake. They were helped by local people, who smuggled supplies to them. The local constable turned a blind eye, but not the Dominion Police, a special force whose job it was to catch evaders. A small posse arrived in Cumberland, headed by Inspector William Devitt with Constable Dan Campbell, a crack shot and superb outdoorsman who had been fired from the British Columbia Provincial Police for extortion.

On the morning of July 27, 1918, Devitt, Campbell, and Constable George Roe headed down Comox Lake, guided by trappers. They went

Ginger Goodwin's funeral in Cumberland.
IMAGE CI 10-001 COURTESY OF CUMBERLAND MUSEUM AND ARCHIVES

to Alone Mountain at the end of the lake. The trappers left the party, and the policemen headed into the bush. Devitt and Roe took one trail, and Campbell another. At 4:30 PM, a shot rang out from Campbell's trail. Devitt and Roe hurried over and found Goodwin's lifeless body.

Campbell claimed he had shot in self-defence when Goodwin raised a rifle toward him. Devitt ordered Campbell back to Cumberland, to surrender to the provincial police.

A preliminary inquiry was held in Victoria to see whether Campbell should stand trial for manslaughter, and the magistrates committed him for trial.

But by law, the final recommendation had to come from a grand jury. Its proceedings were secret, and no record was kept. On October 1, 1918, the jury began hearing witnesses. The next day, they issued their recommendation: Campbell would not go to trial.

Was Goodwin's death a conspiracy? The shooting did not appear to be an ambush, but neither did it seem like self-defence.

And what of Goodwin's legacy? His career was very short, less than two years. His death made him a martyr. Was it justified? Working conditions of a century ago were terrible.

Business owners had little incentive to do anything about working conditions, and governments backed them up. Goodwin's writings on the class struggle, while they seem extreme today, describe the situation very well. He was more moderate than some, and argued for education, organization, and agitation as weapons in the class struggle.

He was also willing to work with government and owners to improve workers' conditions, a position that some on the left denounced. But he also stood up to owners and managers.

There was certainly no justification for him to have been hunted like an animal and killed.

Sir Joseph William Trutch, first Lieutenant-Governor of BC.
IMAGE A-01004 COURTESY OF ROYAL BC MUSEUM, BC ARCHIVES

Sir Joseph Trutch

A FEW YEARS AGO, *The Beaver* asked a panel of historians to name the worst Canadians in history. Among this hall of infamy, there was one name that caught my eye. Joseph Trutch, a leading politician in nineteenth-century British Columbia, was nominated by Daniel Francis. Since I had barely heard of Trutch, I was intrigued. Who was this most infamous of British Columbians?

Joseph Trutch was born in England in 1826. He lived his early years in Jamaica, where his father owned land. After moving back to England, Joseph Trutch graduated from a grammar school and apprenticed as a railway engineer. But he was looking for greater opportunities and so headed to California. He wound up in Illinois, where he was the assistant superintendent of the Illinois and Michigan Canal.

Trutch was always an Englishman at heart, so when he heard of the Fraser River gold rush, he headed to BC. He arrived in 1859 and became involved in surveying and road construction. He won many government contracts and was becoming a wealthy man.

Lady Trutch, wife of Sir Joseph Trutch.
IMAGE A-01708 COURTESY OF ROYAL BC MUSEUM, BC ARCHIVES

Trutch became involved in politics, winning a seat in the colonial legislature in 1861. He became well known to those who ran the colony. In 1864, the governor, James Douglas, decided to retire. The position of chief commissioner of lands and works was vacant, and Douglas, as a parting gesture, recommended Trutch for this post. Doing so was controversial, because Trutch was so heavily involved with government contracts. But he took the position anyway.

Douglas had recommended Trutch because of his experience with surveying and public works. But part of the job was handling Native land policy. Trutch was definitely unsuited for that. His attitude toward Native people can only be described as racist, but he was not alone in his sentiments. Settlers were coming to BC, from Britain and elsewhere, to establish farms and create a new life for themselves. The Natives who had previously occupied the land were a nuisance to them.

James Douglas was very different. He had spent his life in the fur trade, constantly dealing with Native people. The fur trade was dependent on them because they collected the furs. They traded them, with men like Douglas, for the goods they needed.

So important were the Native people to this economy that fair treatment of them was British government policy. The Royal Proclamation of 1763 laid out their rights. It acknowledged that Native people owned the land they had used and occupied. They had "title" to the land, and if the government wanted that "title," it would have to buy it. So the government was obliged to negotiate treaties.

In accordance with this policy, Douglas began to sign treaties with Native groups. From 1850 to 1854, he signed fourteen agreements on Vancouver Island. He thought that their only future was integration with white society, and wanted to prepare them for that.

All this changed in 1864. Douglas retired, and the Native people lost their only friend in government. New governors knew little about them and allowed Joseph Trutch to set land policy. And his policy was to open BC to white settlement.

Trutch began to cut the size of some reserves. He claimed that Douglas had intended only ten acres for each Native family.

Douglas had mentioned ten acres as a minimum. Trutch changed that to a maximum. He also claimed that some reserves were much larger than Douglas intended. This was simply untrue.

Trutch's worst falsification, though, was his denial of Native title. As this was an obvious change to policy, he had to elaborate his view to the governor:

> The title of the Indians in the fee of the public lands . . . has never been acknowledged by the Government, but, on the contrary, is distinctly denied.

How did Trutch get away with it? The answer is he had a willing audience. A settler society was developing that wanted the myth of an empty land. The concept of Native title was highly inconvenient, so it was forgotten as quickly as possible.

In the 1860s, BC was still a Crown colony. With Britain far away, local politicians had free rein with land policy. But not for long; Britain wanted BC to join Confederation. For these local politicians, this posed a problem. The federal government had authority for Native affairs. Also, it was far more generous, acknowledging Native title and creating much larger reserves. Trutch might be forced to do the same.

In 1871, BC decided to join Confederation. Trutch was appointed head of the negotiating team and, luckily for him, the federal

Sir James Douglas.

Gilbert Malcolm Sproat.

government knew little of BC's land policy. Thus BC was able to insert a clause into the agreement that read: "A policy as liberal as that hitherto pursued by the BC government shall be continued by the Dominion Government after the Union." The federal government did not know that BC's policy had been far from liberal. It took them years to realize they'd been hoodwinked.

In 1871, Trutch was appointed BC's first Lieutenant-Governor. At the same time, the federal government was writing treaties with tribes on the Prairies and establishing reserves that had 160 acres of land for each Native family. Naturally, the province's Native people wanted the same. The federal government began to get more involved with them. In 1872, I.W. Powell was appointed as the province's Superintendent of Indian Affairs. He became a source of information the government needed.

Gradually the federal government became more openly critical of BC.

What could not be ignored was rising discontent among Native people. Powell wrote to Ottawa that "If there has not been an Indian War, it is . . . because the Indians have not been sufficiently united." But that was starting to change. In 1874, there was a meeting of 109 chiefs in Hope, some from as far away as Lillooet and Bute Inlet. Native people were overcoming their traditional animosities and uniting in the face of a common enemy.

In response, the federal and provincial governments created, in 1876, the Joint Indian Reserve Commission. Composed of one federal appointee, one provincial one, and one appointed by both governments, this group began a truly serious investigation into Native land needs.

The group did excellent work, interviewing Native people and

Gilbert Malcolm Sproat, in his role as Indian Commissioner on the Fraser River at Yale.
IMAGE A-01771 COURTESY OF ROYAL BC MUSEUM, BC ARCHIVES

doing extensive research. But their work was slow and expensive, and both governments were becoming critical. So in 1878 the commission was reduced to one member.

If the governments were hoping for someone cheaper and less generous, they were wrong. Gilbert Sproat, the remaining commissioner, was a man who had begun to understand and empathize with the Native people. He was even more generous with his reserves.

But that was not all. He began attending major meetings of native chiefs. To the government, this was dangerous encouragement of Native unity. Uprisings were feared. Sproat had to go.

Sproat was forced to resign in 1880. But an Indian Reserves Commissioner was still needed. The government needed a man who could work quickly and award the minimum amount of land, someone who would ask few questions and do what he was told. Joseph Trutch had just the man: his brother-in-law, Peter O'Reilly. O'Reilly was appointed and got to work. Over the next eighteen years he created most of the reserves that still exist today. He consulted little with the Native people and generally kept the reserves to an acceptable minimum. Rarely did any politician find problems with his work. No treaties were signed, and Native title was conveniently forgotten.

Trutch stayed on in Victoria until 1889, when he retired to England. He received a knighthood for his great colonial service, and died in 1904.

Trutch left a dark legacy. His denial of Native title, and other legitimate claims, poisoned relations between the white and Native people of BC and led to more than a century of conflict.

Native people, though, have struggled back. They have never forgotten their right of title and have campaigned for its recognition. The process of negotiating treaties has begun.

No one imagines it will be easy. But because Trutch was unwilling to sign treaties, he left the field open. Native people negotiate by today's standards, not by those of the nineteenth century. If he had written treaties, Trutch would have given the Native people a pittance. Now they will receive much more. Who would have imagined that Trutch, in the end, would actually help Native people?

A view of Victoria harbour, by W.J. Phillips.

The Rise and Fall of Francis Rattenbury

The Rise of Young Mr. Rattenbury

THE ARCHITECTURE OF FRANCIS RATTENBURY practically defines the city of Victoria. Although he died nearly three-quarters of a century ago, his Parliament Buildings and Empress Hotel still represent the city in the eyes of locals and visitors alike.

Scattered throughout the city are other examples of his genius. The Crystal Gardens was built to his initial design. His own home on Beach Drive (now Glenlyon Norfolk School) is a local landmark for residential architecture. Many more buildings could be listed.

But architecture was only part of his life. As a town planner, he was far ahead of his time and had a particularly strong effect on the development of Oak Bay. As a businessman, he had a hectic career and made some shrewd investments, along with some that failed. He also made contributions as a politician and philanthropist. But it was an event in his personal life that led to his undoing. He had an affair with a much younger woman and badly mistreated his wife. The outcome of this scandal was far-reaching.

Rattenbury was born in England in 1867. He had family

connections to an architectural firm and at age eighteen joined the firm as an articling student, spending several years there, learning his trade. He was an ambitious young man and realized that Canada had greater possibilities for him than England did, especially a new city like Vancouver. So he set sail, arriving in Vancouver in 1892.

His first major commission was a house for Gustav Roedde in Vancouver's West End. (The house is now a museum). But he soon got wind of a far bigger prize. A new provincial legislature was to be built in Victoria, and architects were being invited to compete for the job.

Rattenbury entered the contest with drawings emphasizing the beauty and dignity of the building. But he also employed some clever tactics to help his cause. Submissions had to be anonymous. Realizing the political advantages of being a local resident, he signed his entry "BC Resident." The judges picked him as a finalist. On the second submission, he continued to emphasize his local status, and used the nom de plume "For Our Queen and Province." He won the prize. His great architectural ability and clever tactics were to become hallmarks of his career.

This approach brought him great fame and success, but not without cost. Sometimes he was not scrupulous in the methods he used, and he made many enemies in the process.

Over the next few years, Rattenbury's architectural career blossomed. He was particularly good at designing buildings with a bold, striking presence. This was what business and government leaders frequently wanted, and so it led to some impressive commissions. He designed several branches for the Bank of Montreal, including a fine one on Government Street. For the government he did several court houses, including the one in Vancouver that is now the Vancouver Art Gallery. But his biggest customer of all was the Canadian Pacific Railway (CPR).

Francis Mawson Rattenbury.

Official opening of the new Legislative Buildings, 1898.
IMAGE A-02647 COURTESY OF ROYAL BC MUSEUM, BC ARCHIVES

Rattenbury was an obvious architect for the CPR to use, because he had shown that he had great ability in designing château-style buildings, which was the company's signature style. As well, he had designed the BC Legislative Buildings, which was the most impressive building in Western Canada. So the CPR appointed him the architect of its western division. He did not disappoint. He went on to create Mount Stephen House in the Canadian Rockies and designed additions to many other CPR properties. He also designed the CPR Steamship Terminal beside Victoria's Inner Harbour and, most impressive of all, the Empress Hotel.

In the Empress Hotel he did more than create a fine building. He was designing an entrance to Victoria. He knew that the Empress would fit in with the BC Legislative Buildings and the CPR Steamship Terminal to create an outstanding symbol of the city. The future for Victoria, as he saw it, was tourism, and the city needed a design that would greet tourists impressively. Ideas like these were ahead of their time, and it was only in the late twentieth century that local leaders started to adopt the same approaches.

What Rattenbury did for Oak Bay was equally impressive. He appreciated what an asset the Victoria Golf Club was to Oak Bay. When it was threatened with development, he ran for reeve of Oak Bay on a platform of stopping the development. He won the election, and the threat receded. But he knew that more green space was needed. He directed the Oak Bay council to buy the land that became Willows Park. He also gave the municipality land of his own. He had bought Mary Tod Island (known locally as Jimmy Chicken Island) in the early 1900s to make sure it was not developed. By the 1920s he realized that its best use was as a park, so he gave it to the municipality.

Finally, he was also advisory architect for the Uplands subdivision in Oak Bay. Uplands had been laid out in a sensitive, park-like manner, and Rattenbury was appointed architect to make sure it stayed that way. He did his job well. Uplands, like the rest of Oak Bay, is still one of the most beautiful residential areas in Canada. Rattenbury is largely responsible for this.

Rattenbury was always as much a businessman as an architect. He was usually wise and careful in his investments, but two of them almost ruined him.

Even before he finished the Legislative Buildings he became fascinated with the Yukon gold rush. With his friend, Calgary shipping magnate Pat Burns, Rattenbury invested in shipping meat to the Yukon. The success of this venture fired his interest. He saw that what was really needed was a fleet of riverboats to go from Lake Bennett to Dawson. Raising the capital, he set up the Lake Bennett and Klondike Navigation Company and built the boats. Next, to ensure its viability, he negotiated a shipping contract with his friend Pat Burns.

But Rattenbury still had to prove that travel to the Yukon was now easy and reliable. To do so, he decided to go there himself. He had just married, so he and his bride, Florence, spent their honeymoon hiking the Chilkoot Pass. When they reached Lake Bennett, they took one of his steamers to Dawson. Business was booming in Dawson, and everything looked rosy for his investments.

But Rattenbury should have been more wary. Gold rushes in the past had always been ephemeral, and the Yukon gold rush was no exception. He made even more Klondike investments, but then circumstances suddenly changed. A new gold strike was discovered in Nome, Alaska, and Dawson began to empty. Hurriedly, Rattenbury rid himself of his investments, but it was too late. He took a financial beating.

His next big investment looked secure, but ultimately was not. He left the CPR in 1906 to take an active role in a new railway, the Grand Trunk Pacific. He was the chief architect for its new hotels, and invested heavily in land on its northern route. The chief proponent of this railway was its president, Charles Melville Hays. When he drowned in the sinking of the *Titanic* in 1912, much of the company's force went with him. When war was declared in 1914, the company's fate was sealed. It went bankrupt a few years later and was taken over by the government. Rattenbury built little for the company, and his land was now almost worthless.

Not only did his railway venture collapse, but demand for Rattenbury's style of architecture died as well. Faced with changing tastes, he realized his career as an architect was essentially over. By

"Lechinihl," Francis Rattenbury's home on Beach Drive.
IMAGE D-03002 COURTESY OF ROYAL BC MUSEUM, BC ARCHIVES

the beginning of the war, he still had a commission to renovate the Legislative Buildings. That and his investments were what he lived on. This lasted several years and might well have gone on indefinitely.

The city, however, decided to intervene. City leaders in the early 1920s wanted to build an indoor swimming pool. They had tried to do this in 1912, but a referendum on the issue had been defeated. Suspecting that poor design was the problem, the city turned to Rattenbury for help. He obliged them by designing what was really an amusement palace. It was named the Crystal Gardens, in memory of Britain's famed Crystal Palace. The CPR, in return for substantial tax breaks, agreed to finance its construction. So in December 1923, a second referendum passed overwhelmingly.

To celebrate Rattenbury's success, a dinner was held in his honour at the Empress Hotel. After much goodwill and cheering, he retired to the lounge to have a cigar. There he met Alma Pakenham, and as Terry Reksten says in his book *Rattenbury*, "his life was never the same again."

Decline and Fall

When Francis Rattenbury married in 1898, people were surprised at his choice. He had just built the BC Legislative Buildings, making him BC's most celebrated architect. He had many projects on the go and was a highly ambitious man. A society lady would have been an obvious choice and would have furthered his ambitions.

Instead, he married Florence Nunn, who was quiet and plain, and from very humble origins. He had known her for several years and was presumably very comfortable with her. But to many, it seemed a strange match.

In the years to come, the apparent mismatch began to prove true. When Rattenbury went out socializing, he went alone. Florence pottered around the house and rarely entertained. She grew increasingly stout, prim, and dull. The gulf between them widened, and antipathy developed into outright animosity. By the onset of the war, they were no longer speaking to each other.

The war years marked a bad time for Rattenbury. Demand for his style of architecture was waning, and his Grand Trunk Railway investments had been a disaster. This, combined with a miserable home life, was making him turn to drink. He had never been abstemious, but his previous drinking had been social. Now he would consume a bottle every night alone. Much of the time he was depressed. His renovations of the legislature kept him financially afloat, but otherwise he was in a bad way. The Crystal Gardens project of the 1920s saved him, not only reviving his career, but also leading him to new love.

Alma Pakenham was in Victoria to give a concert. A fine pianist, she had just finished a recital at the Empress on the night of Rattenbury's fete to celebrate the Crystal Gardens project. In the distance she heard loud choruses of "For He's a Jolly Good Fellow." Curious, she wandered in the direction of the sound. There she saw the man of the hour. A friend who was there and happened to know Rattenbury introduced them, and Alma and Rattenbury's friendship began.

Alma Pakenham (née Clarke) was born in Kamloops in 1895. A lively, vivacious child, she showed great musical ability early on. So gifted was she that at age eighteen, she played two different concertos with the Toronto Symphony Orchestra. She was also a composer of songs. In 1914 she married Caledon Dolling, who was killed two years later at the Battle of the Somme. (She herself served as a war nurse with great distinction.) After the war she married Thomas Pakenham, of the literary Longford family. A son, Christopher, was born, but the marriage ended disastrously. She moved to Vancouver, and resumed her concert career. It was on the night of one of these concerts that she met Rattenbury.

Alma moved to Victoria, and a relationship with Rattenbury quickly developed. Both were starved for passion, especially Rattenbury. He was not interested in being discreet, and his lover was never one to hide her feelings, either. Soon they were the talk of Victoria.

Many were angry at the way Mrs. Rattenbury was being treated. Rattenbury wanted a divorce and was determined to get it. When his wife refused, he repeatedly harassed her. He moved furniture out of their house and cut the power. When that failed to move her, he began entertaining Alma in their house, forcing his wife upstairs while he did so. Eventually he got his way. Or so he thought.

Alma Rattenbury.

What he was not prepared for was social ostracization. His behaviour was considered so outrageous that public respect for him evaporated. Alma was equally unprepared for the reaction. Growing up a musical prodigy, she had always been feted and her faults overlooked. Now she was seen as a bewitching temptress, a disrupter of family life. In addition, she was accused of taking drugs and introducing Rattenbury to them. Although she and Rattenbury married and had a son, they were never socially accepted.

The final break came in 1929. Florence Rattenbury died, but the bitterness remained. The children would have nothing to do with their father. Rattenbury saw that reconciliation was impossible and decided to leave Victoria. In December he and Alma set sail for England.

They settled in Bournemouth, a seaside resort town. With its population of ex-colonials and retirees, it was much like Victoria. The choice was undoubtedly Rattenbury's. Alma was, after all, not yet forty, and she still had career hopes. She probably would have preferred the bustling life of London, but she was always agreeable and willing to go along with Rattenbury's wishes.

Getting along with Rattenbury, though, was getting harder. He had not realized how dependent he had been on personal status and prestige. He also needed challenging work, of which Bournemouth offered none. There he was just one of many ex-colonials with interesting stories to tell. Nobody knew of his career in Victoria, and nobody cared. No one wanted him as an architect. His financial resources were rapidly diminishing. He sank into alcoholism and depression.

He became a shadow of the man he once was. Along with alcoholism and depression came another development: sexual impotence. He was becoming an old man, while his wife was still young and beautiful. Perhaps unsurprisingly, she took a lover.

George Percy Stoner was just seventeen when he went to work for the Rattenburys. They needed a chauffeur and someone who could do various odd jobs. He seemed to fit the job perfectly—perhaps too perfectly. Alma had not sought out a lover, but she succumbed to temptation and seduced him.

Stoner, though, was young and naive. Still only in his late teens, he had little experience with the world. Alma, by contrast, had been married three times and was old enough to be his mother. The gulf between them was enormous. Emotions were welling up in Stoner that surprised Alma. He became jealous of her husband, and could not cope with a love triangle. The situation was a time-bomb waiting to explode. Alma precipitated things. She took Stoner to London for an intimate weekend alone and lavished expensive gifts on him, but on their return home, he became just a servant again. When she and her husband decided to go on an overnight trip, Stoner went wild. He said she would be sleeping with Rattenbury again and would renew their marital relationship. Alma denied it, but to no avail. Stoner had reached the breaking point.

Exactly what happened next will never be known for sure. The night before Alma and Rattenbury were to leave on their trip, they were playing cards. She excused herself at 9:30 PM to go and pack. A little later she went to bed, and Stoner joined her. At about 10:30 they heard loud groans from below. Alma rushed out, to discover Rattenbury covered in blood. He had been attacked. Alma's servant, Irene, appeared and immediately phoned for a doctor. Two doctors came, and Rattenbury, still alive, was sent to a hospital. They could also see it was deliberate assault and called the police.

The police came and questioned everyone, particularly Alma. After many wild and contradictory statements, fuelled more and more

Wedding photograph of Mrs. Francis Mawson Rattenbury.

by alcohol, she confessed she had done it and was arrested for assault. But later Stoner admitted to Irene that he had done it. In the meantime, Rattenbury died. The police, acting on Irene's information, arrested Stoner. Both he and Alma were now charged with murder.

It was a sensational trial at the Old Bailey. The public lined up for hours to get a seat, and the press had a field day. The main feature was Alma's testimony. She had recanted her confession and pleaded not guilty. Despite intense questioning she could not be discredited. In a low, rich voice, she answered all the questions well and seemed credible.

Her testimony, though she did not intend it to, put the blame on Stoner. As Stoner did not testify, the direction of the case was clear. The jury acquitted Alma and convicted Stoner. He was sentenced to hang.

Alma was distraught. She was put in a nursing home, talked incessantly of Stoner, and frequently mentioned suicide.

After a few days, however, she improved dramatically. And then one night she had an unknown visitor, a woman who stayed several hours and then left. She insisted that Alma come with her, despite protests from the nurse. The two did go; then Alma returned later, alone.

What was this meeting about? No one will ever know for sure, but notes that Alma made, found afterwards, provide a clue. The woman had apparently persuaded her that she could not save Stoner from hanging.

The next day Alma borrowed two pounds from a nurse. With it she bought a knife. Later that night she was seen on the bank of the River Avon, swinging her arms wildly and then falling into the river. When her body was retrieved, her wounds revealed that she had stabbed herself to death.

The identity of the woman and what she said to Alma remain unknown, but if the visitor goaded Alma into suicide, her words

Francis and Alma Rattenbury, with their son John. This picture appeared
in the local press after Mrs. Rattenbury was charged with murder.
DAILY COLONIST, APRIL 25, 1935

had the desired effect. Seeking a reprieve for Stoner while his lover
was still alive would have been hopeless. The thought of Alma and
Stoner together again, even after many years, was morally intoler-
able to the public. She was seen as an evil seductress who had led
him astray.

But with Alma dead, it was decided that something could be done
for Stoner. A campaign was launched, and soon there was mount-
ing public pressure to commute his sentence. The Home Secretary
was presented with a huge petition. He deferred all comment until
legal appeals had run their course. Then he made an announcement:
Stoner's sentence would be commuted to "penal servitude for life."

In the end Stoner served only seven years of his sentence. He was released to the army to fight in the war. After the war he faded into private life. He died in the year 2000, less than a mile away from where Alma had died by the Avon.

And what of the Rattenbury sons? Both, according to the magazine *Dorset Life*, went on to "lead happy family lives and have successful professional careers." John Rattenbury, the son of Francis and Alma, is the only one still alive. He became an architect and worked with Frank Lloyd Wright at Taliesen West. In 1998 John Rattenbury was invited back to Victoria. The occasion was the one hundredth anniversary of the legislature, his father's building.

The festivities were a revelation for John. He could see the old scandals were forgotten and his father honoured once again. Throughout Victoria were his father's achievements. Oak Bay in particular had been shaped by Rattenbury. Later in the day John was allowed to see that for himself. He was taken to "Lechinihl," the house his father had built and where John had been born. The house, now Glenlyon-Norfolk School, is a landmark in local architecture. The experience was very moving for John. He later described it as a personal "closing of a circle, and the highlight of my life."

Great things had been predicted of Francis Rattenbury when, as a young man, he had built the Legislative Buildings. He went on to lead a turbulent life, full of failures as well as triumphs. But he was a craftsman of great skill and knew what he wanted to achieve. His art remains as a testament to his vision.

Yours truly, Fra. Rattenbury

Further Reading

Caddy the Cadborosaurus

The basic book on Caddy is *Cadborosaurus: Survivor of the Deep*, by Paul H. LeBlond and Edward L. Bousfield. Their book covers all aspects of the Caddy story and contains useful appendices, such as a listing of all recorded cadborosaurus sightings. It also has many citations of original stories in local newspapers, which are available on microfilm at the central branch of the GVPL. Also available at the library is the excellent article on Hubert Evans by Howard White, in *Raincoast Chronicles Six/Ten*. White shows why the Evans sighting is so valuable, and incidentally focuses attention on an important writer.

Other books of interest are *Basking Sharks: The Slaughter of BC's Gentle Giants*, by Scott Wallace and Brian Gisborne; *Monsters of the Sea*, by Richard Ellis; *In the Wake of the Sea-Serpents*, by Bernard Heuvelmans; and *The Ghost with Trembling Wings: Science, Wishful Thinking and the Search for Lost Species*. For people wishing to read about sea monsters from a mildly sceptical viewpoint, the last book has a fascinating chapter, "Cruising the Crypto-Fringe."

The April Ghost of the Victoria Golf Links

The April Ghost of the Victoria Golf Links, by Charles Lillard and Robin Skelton.
    Central Library Local History Room
A Gathering of Ghosts, by Robin Skelton and Jean Kozocari.
    Central Library Local History Room
Ghost Stories of British Columbia, by Jo-Anne Christensen.
    Central Library Local History Room and other locations of the GVPL

The Lepers of D'Arcy Island

A Measure of Value: The Story of the D'Arcy Island Leper Colony, by C.J. Yorath.
A Dream of Islands, by Philip Teece.
From China to Canada: A History of the Chinese Communities in Canada, by Harry Con et al.
There is also a clipping file in the GVPL's Local History Room, under the heading "D'Arcy Island."

Chinatown Myths and Realities

Forbidden City within Victoria, by David Chuen-yan Lai.
Chinatowns: Towns within Cities in Canada, by David Chuen-yan Lai.
Chinese and Japanese Immigration: Report of the Royal Commission, 1902.
    Central Library Local History Room

The Local History Room of the GVPL contains many resources about Victoria's Chinese heritage, including old newspaper clippings and microfilms of local papers from 1858.

Jimmy Chicken

The GVPL's Local History Room has an extensive clipping file on Jimmy Chicken (or "Chickens," as some sources name him). Included are two lengthy articles published in the Victoria newspapers following his death in 1901. Philip Teece's book *A Dream of Islands* has a sketch of the graveyard on Chatham Island, where Jimmy Chicken is presumed to have been buried. Grant Keddie's *Songhees Pictorial: A History of the Songhees People as Seen by Outsiders* presents a historical view of the Songhees people.

The Sea Wolf

Captain Alex MacLean: Jack London's Sea Wolf, by Don MacGillivray.

The Vagabond Fleet: A Chronicle of the North Pacific Sealing Schooner Trade, by Peter Murray.

The War against the Seals: A History of the North American Seal Fishery, by Briton Cooper Busch.

The Sea Wolf, by Jack London.

The Local History Room of the GVPL has a biography clipping file on Alex MacLean under the heading "MacLean, Alexander."

Brother XII

Brother XII: The Strange Odyssey of a 20th Century Prophet and His Quest for a New World, by John Oliphant.

This is easily the best book on Brother XII. The author spent over ten years researching it and interviewed many of the people involved. The book, however, lacks footnotes or a bibliography detailing his sources.

Brother XII: The Devil of DeCourcy Island, by Ronald MacIsaac et al.

This is a short and not very well researched book. It was written to defend Brother XII from the sensational stories in the newspapers, but is essentially an apology for him. The writing style is dry, and the book reads like a lawyer's brief.

Canada's False Prophet: The Notorious Brother Twelve, by Herbert Emmerson Wilson.

This book purports to be a biography of Brother XII by his brother Herbert Emmerson Wilson. In fact, according to John Robert Colombo, the real author is a hack writer named Thomas P. Kelley. There was also a Herbert Emerson (single "m") Wilson who, according to the UBC Library's Special Collections website was a convicted safe-cracker and murderer, as well as being the purported author of this book. Since this Wilson was born in Canada and Edward Arthur Wilson was born in England, there is hardly any likelihood there was a real connection between them. One possibility is that this book was cooked up by Kelley and Herbert Emerson Wilson to cash in on Brother XII's notoriety. In any case, it should be read with caution.

As well as these books, the GVPL has an extensive clipping file on Brother XII. The stories are, for the most part, very sensational and predate the researches of MacIsaac (et al.) and Oliphant, and so should also be regarded with caution.

The Yuquot Whalers' Shrine

Captured Heritage: The Scramble for Northwest Coast Artifacts, by Douglas Cole.
The Yuquot Whalers' Shrine, by Aldona Jonaitis.
From the Land of the Totem Poles: The Northwest Coast Indian Art Collection at the American Museum of Natural History, by Aldona Jonaitis.
Chiefly Feasts: The Enduring Kwakiutl Potlatch, edited by Aldona Jonaitis. This book is particularly useful for its essay on George Hunt.

The Pig War

The Pig War, by Keith A. Murray.
San Juan: The Powder-Keg Island, by Jo Bailey-Cummings and Al Cummings.
Outpost of Empire: The Royal Marines and the Joint Occupation of San Juan Island, by Mike Vouri.
The Pig War: The Journal of William A. Peck Jr., by William A. Peck Jr.
The Local History Room of the GVPL has a clipping file on the Pig War.

The Vancouver / Camelford Affair

A Voyage of Discovery to the North Pacific Ocean and Round the World, 1791–1795 (four volumes), by George Vancouver, edited by W. Kaye Lamb.
The Half-Mad Lord: Thomas Pitt, 2nd Baron Camelford (1775–1804), by Nikolai Tolstoy.
On Stormy Seas: The Triumphs and Torments of Captain George Vancouver, by B. Guild Gillespie.
The Interwoven Lives of George Vancouver, Archibald Menzies, Joseph Whidbey and Peter Puget: Exploring the Pacific Northwest Coast, by John M. Naish.

In the Land of the Head Hunters

Edward S. Curtis in the Land of the War Canoes: A Pioneer Cinematographer in the Pacific Northwest, by Bill Holm and George Irving Quimby.
Edward S. Curtis: Coming to Light, by Anne Makepeace.

Edward Sheriff Curtis: Visions of a Vanishing Race, by Florence Curtis Graybill and Victor Boesen.

In the Land of the War Canoes: A Drama of Kwakiutl Indian Life on the Northwest Coast [DVD]. Website: www.curtisfilm.rutgers.edu.

Also, there were several articles on the Curtis film and the Kwakwaka'wakw in the *Vancouver Sun*. They were published in the period leading up to, and after, the screening of the restored version of *In the Land of the Head Hunters* on June 22, 2008. These are easily accessed on the Canadian Newstand database to which the GVPL subscribes.

John Jewitt

The GVPL owns copies of several editions of Jewitt's *Narrative*. These include, in the Local History Room, a second edition from 1815. Also there is an edition from 1896 with an introduction by Robert Brown, an early explorer of Vancouver Island's Interior. Copies of some later editions are in circulation or in the Local History Room. A fictional account of Jewitt's life, titled *Rivers of Rain*, and a pamphlet on his later life, called appropriately "Later Life of John R. Jewitt," are both held in the Local History Room. A few years ago a reprint edition of Jewitt's original *Journal* was published. Both circulating and Local History Room copies of it are available. It's interesting to read the *Journal* first, then the *Narrative*, to see how the story evolved. A newspaper clipping file on Jewitt is in the Local History Room.

The Battle of the Bishops

Of these records, two unusual items (housed in the GVPL's Local History Room) are a typed manuscript reminiscence of Bishop Cridge by Edgar Fawcett, and a rare (and very fragile!) pamphlet, published in 1875, giving a full account of the Cridge trial.

Mifflin Wistar Gibbs

Go Do Some Great Thing: The Black Pioneers of British Columbia, by Crawford Kilian.

The chapter "A Miniature Race War" in *The Passing of a Race and More Tales of Western Life*, by D.W. Higgins.

The University of Victoria Library has a copy of Gibbs' autobiography: *Shadow and Light: An Autobiography*, by Mifflin Wistar Gibbs.

The GVPL's Local History Room has two relevant clipping files: "Gibbs, Mifflin W." and "Blacks in BC."

Amor De Cosmos

Although relatively little has been written about De Cosmos, a strange and fascinating man, a biography by George Woodcock is in the Local History Room, which also has a clipping file on his life.

Ginger Goodwin

Fighting for Dignity: The Ginger Goodwin Story, by Roger Stonebanks.

Ginger: The Life and Death of Albert Goodwin, by Susan Mayse.

Rebel Life: The Life and Times of Robert Gosden, Revolutionary, Mystic, Labour Spy, by Mark Leier.

This book has an interesting essay on the Goodwin case.

A clipping file on Ginger Goodwin is housed in the GVPL's Local History Room.

Sir Joseph Trutch

Making Native Space: Colonialism, Resistance and Reserves in British Columbia, by Cole Harris.

Aboriginal Peoples and Politics: The Indian Land Question in British Columbia, 1849–1989, by Paul Tennant.

Peter O'Reilly: The Rise of a Reluctant Immigrant, by Lynne Stonier-Newman.

"Joseph Trutch and Indian Land Policy," by Robin Fisher, in *British Columbia: Historical Readings*, compiled and edited by W. Peter Ward and Robert A.J. McDonald.

There is also a clipping file on Sir Joseph Trutch in the Local History Room.

The Rise and Fall of Francis Rattenbury

Rattenbury, by Terry Reksten.

Francis Rattenbury and British Columbia: Architecture and Challenge in the Imperial Age, by Anthony Barrett and Rhodri Windsor Liscombe.

Murder at the Villa Madeira: The Rattenbury Murder, by Sir David Napley.

Tragedy in Three Voices: The Rattenbury Murder, by Sir Michael Havers et. al.

Central Library Local History Room

Cause Celebre: A Play, by Terence Rattigan.

Central Library Local History Room

In addition to these books, an extensive clipping file on Francis Rattenbury is available in the GVPL's Local History Room.